ACROSS THE UNIVERSE

ISBN: 978-1-61774-241-5

HAL•LEONARD®
CORPORATION

7777 W. BLUEMOUND RD. P.O. BOX 13819 MILWAUKEE, WI 53213

Visit Hal Leonard Online at
www.halleonard.com

GIRL

Words and Music by JOHN LENNON
and PAUL McCARTNEY

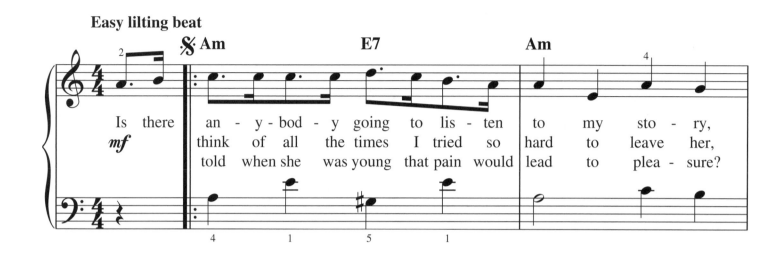

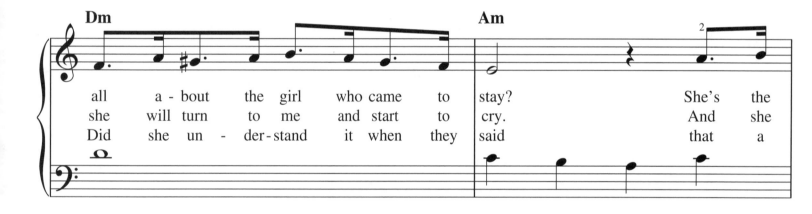

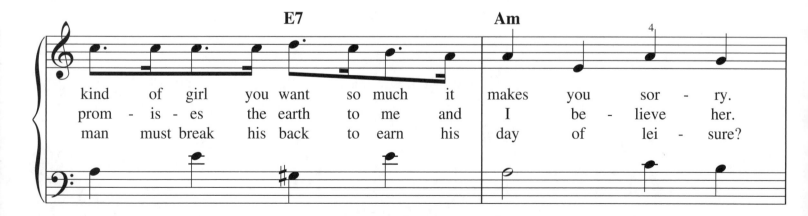

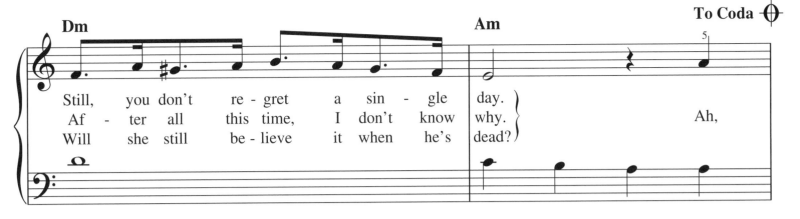

Dm ... Am ... To Coda

Still, you don't re - gret a sin - gle day.
Af - ter all this time, I don't know why.
Will she still be - lieve it when he's dead?

Ah,

C   Em/B   F6/A   G7   C   Em/B

girl, _____

girl,   girl. _____

1.
F6/A   G

2.
F6/A   G7

When I

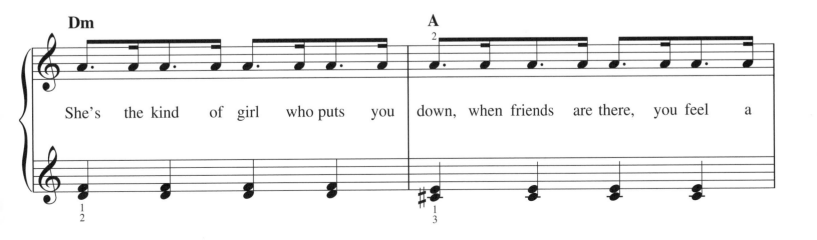

Dm   A

She's the kind of girl who puts you down, when friends are there, you feel a

4

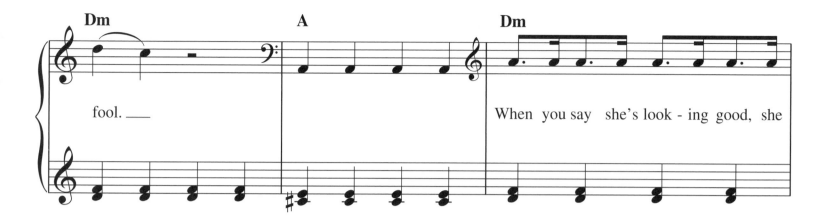

Dm / **A** / **Dm**

fool. ___

When you say she's look - ing good, she

A / **Dm** / **F**

acts as if it's un - der - stood. She's | cool, ___ ooh, ___ | ooh, ___ ooh. ___

cresc.

C / **Em/B** / **F6/A** / **G7** / **C** / **Em/B**

Girl, _____

p

girl, girl. ___

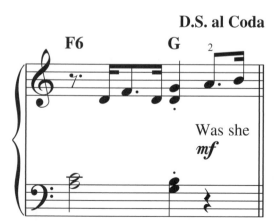

F6 / **G**

Was she

mf

D.S. al Coda

CODA

Repeat and Fade

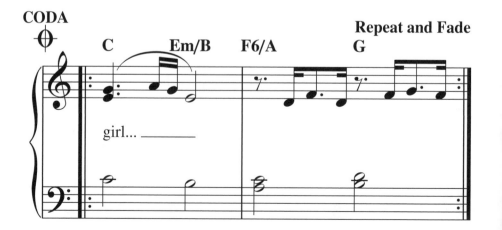

C / **Em/B** / **F6/A** / **G**

girl... ___

IT WON'T BE LONG

Words and Music by JOHN LENNON
and PAUL McCARTNEY

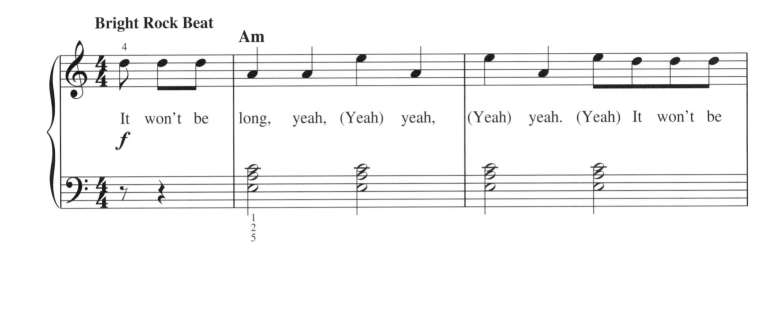

It won't be long, yeah, (Yeah) yeah, (Yeah) yeah. (Yeah) It won't be

long, _ yeah, (Yeah) yeah, (Yeah) yeah. (Yeah) It won't be long, yeah, (Yeah) till

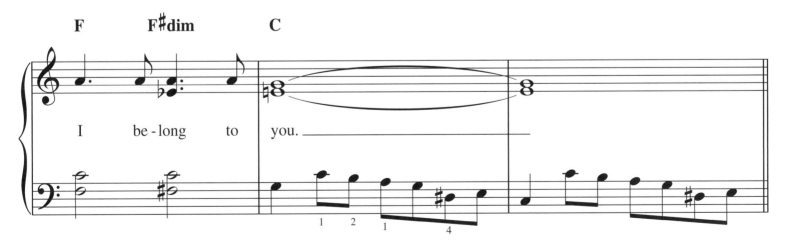

I be-long to you. _

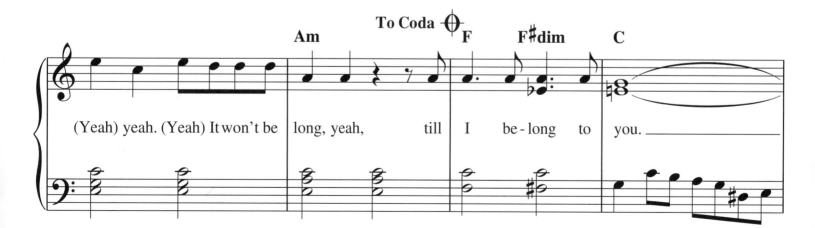

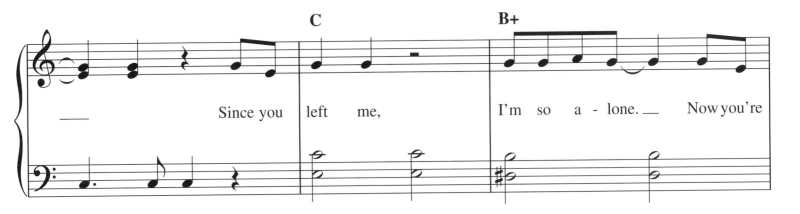

Since you left me, I'm so a-lone.__ Now you're

com-ing, you're com-ing on home.__ I'll be good like I

know I should, you're com-ing home! You're com-ing home!_____

home!__ So,

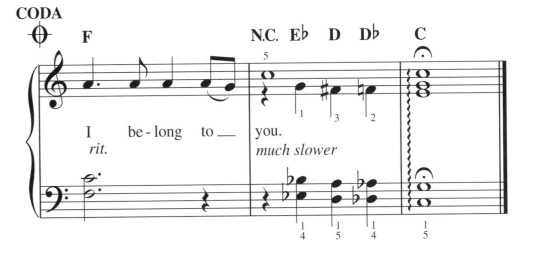

I be-long to __ you.

LET IT BE

Words and Music by JOHN LENNON
and PAUL McCARTNEY

Slowly, in 2

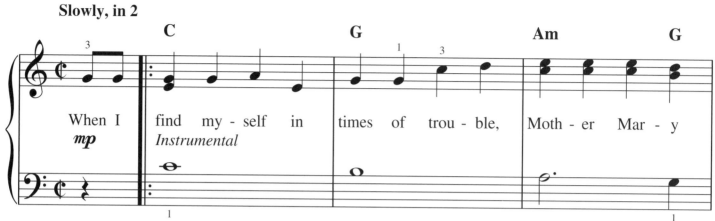

When I find my-self in times of trou-ble, Moth-er Mar-y
mp
Instrumental

With pedal

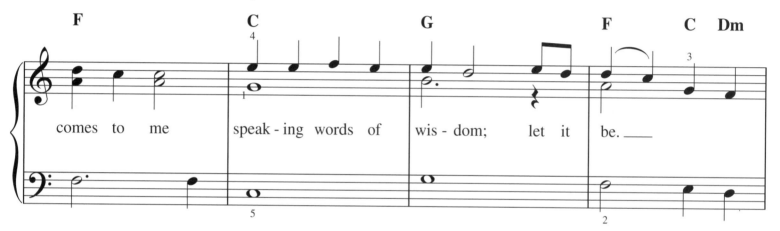

comes to me speak-ing words of wis-dom; let it be. ___

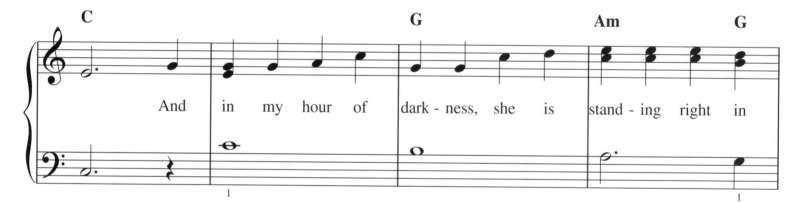

And in my hour of dark-ness, she is stand-ing right in

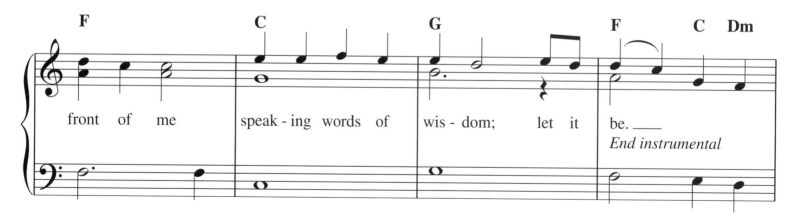

front of me speak-ing words of wis-dom; let it be. ___
End instrumental

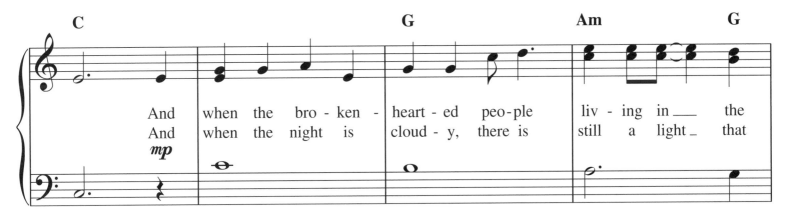

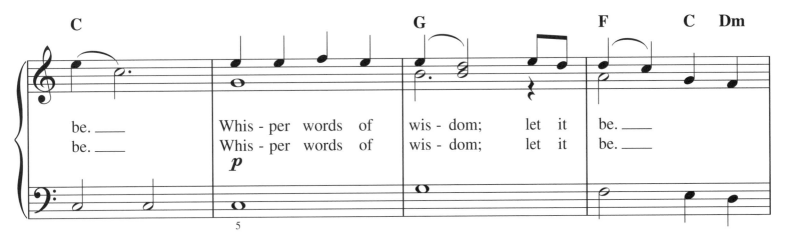

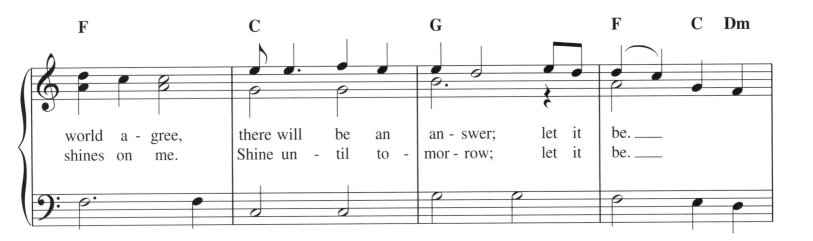

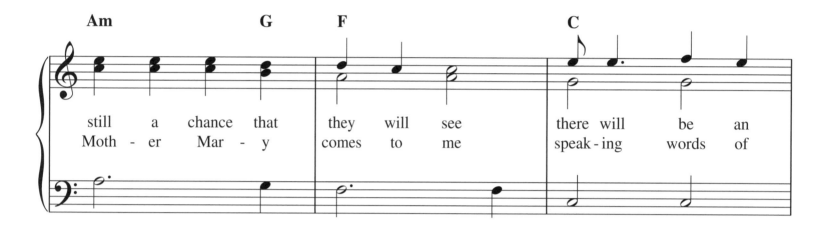

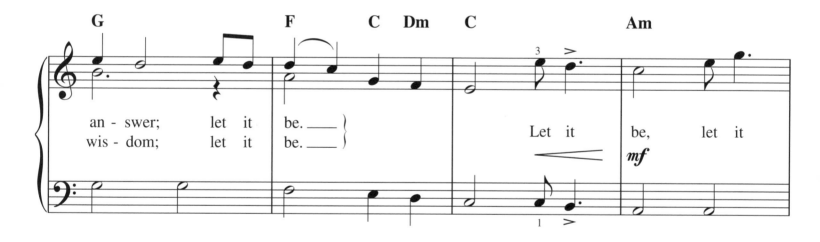

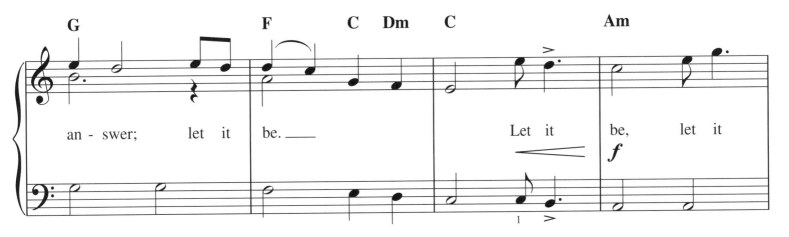

an - swer;   let it   be. ____   Let it   be,   let it

be, ____   let it   be, ____   let it   be.   Whis - per words of / There will be an

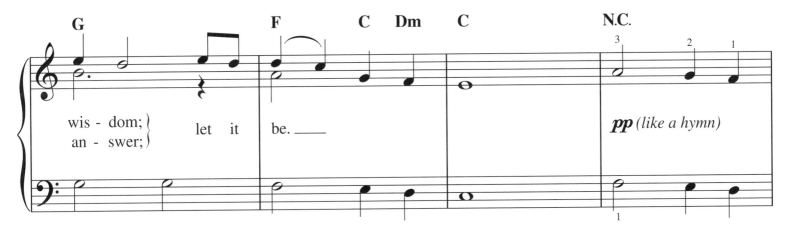

wis - dom; / an - swer;   let it   be. ____   *pp* (like a hymn)

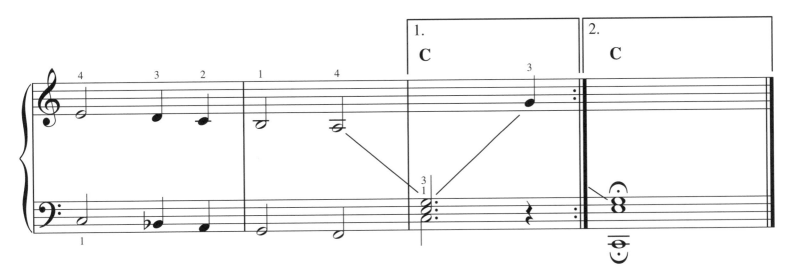

HOLD ME TIGHT

Words and Music by JOHN LENNON
and PAUL McCARTNEY

Moderately

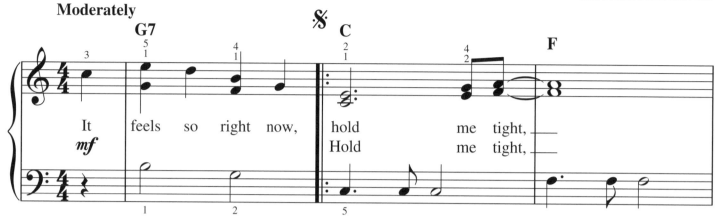

It feels so right now, hold me tight, ___
Hold me tight, ___

tell me I'm the on-ly one, and then I might ___
let me go on lov-ing you to - night, to - night, ___

___ nev-er be the lone-ly one. So ___
___ mak-ing love to on-ly you.

hold me tight ___ to - night, to - night, ___ it's

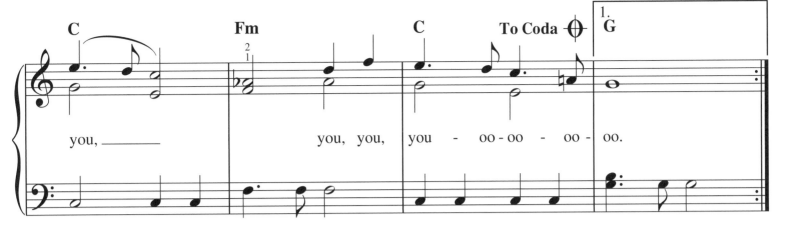

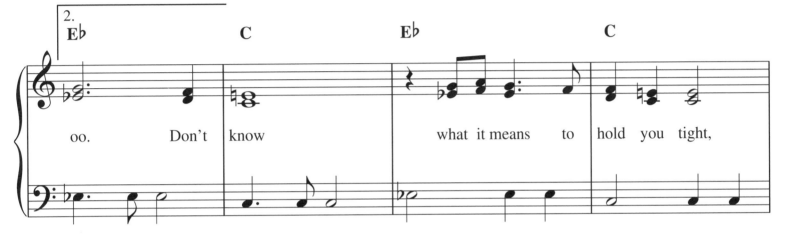

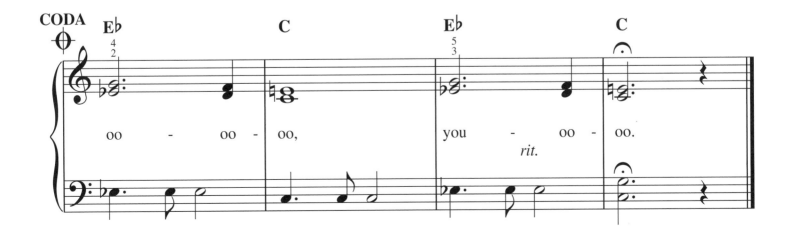

ALL MY LOVING

Words and Music by JOHN LENNON
and PAUL McCARTNEY

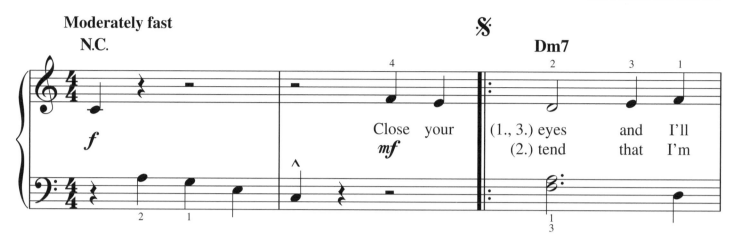

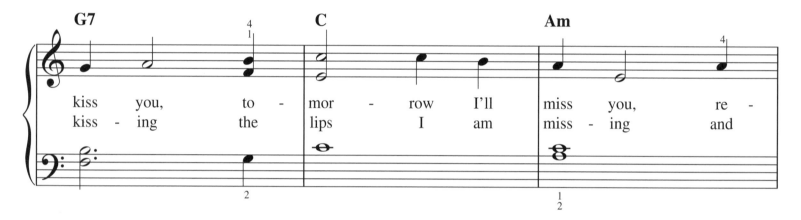

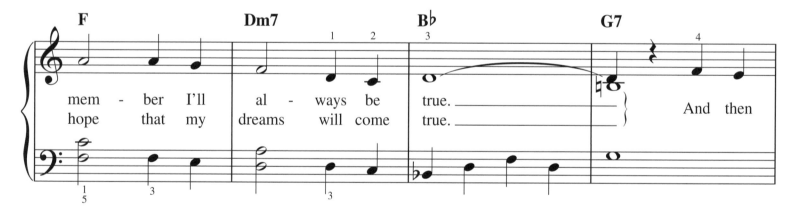

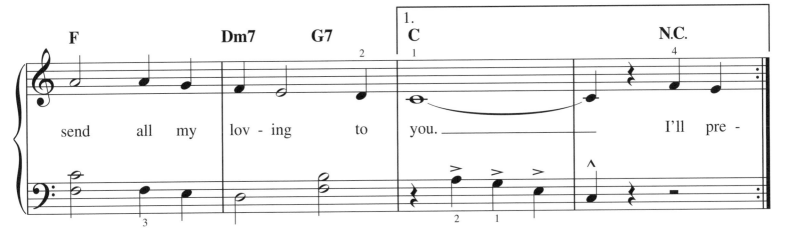

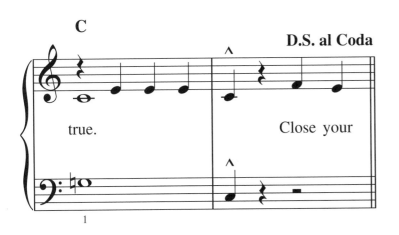

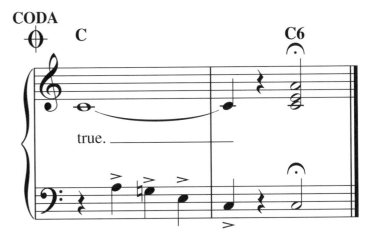

I WANT TO HOLD YOUR HAND

Words and Music by JOHN LENNON
and PAUL McCARTNEY

With a steady Rock beat

Oh yeah, I'll _____ tell you some - thing
please _____ say to me _____

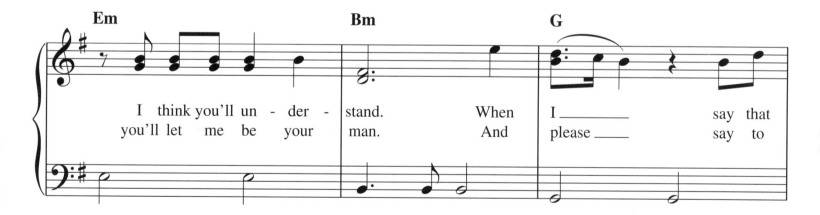

I think you'll un - der - stand. When
you'll let me be your man. And

I _____ say that
please _____ say to

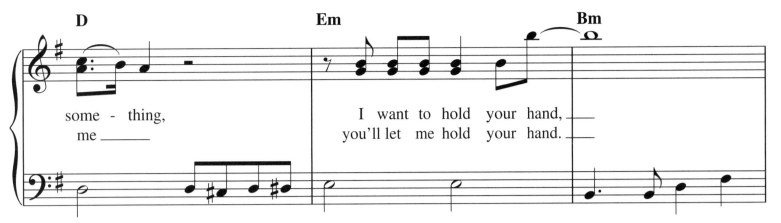

some - thing,
me _____

I want to hold your hand, ____
you'll let me hold your hand. ____

I want to hold your
Now let me hold your

hand, _____
hand, _____

I want to hold your
I want to hold your

1.

hand.   Oh, ___

2.

hand.

And when I

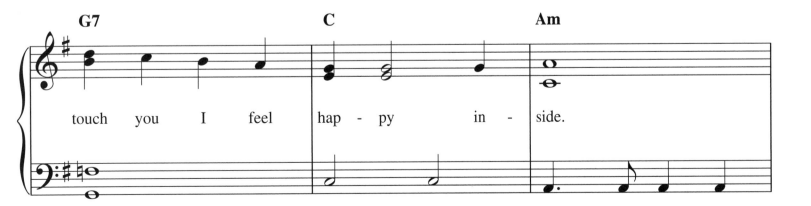

touch you I feel   hap - py   in - side.

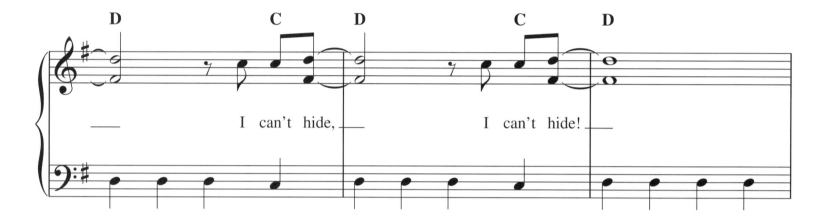

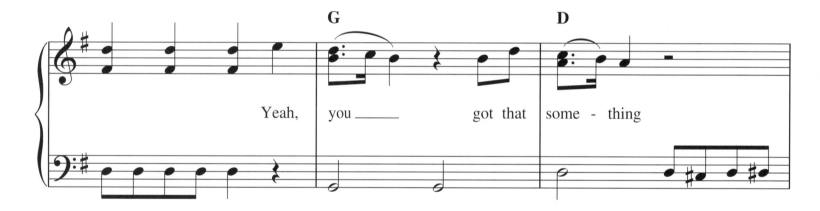

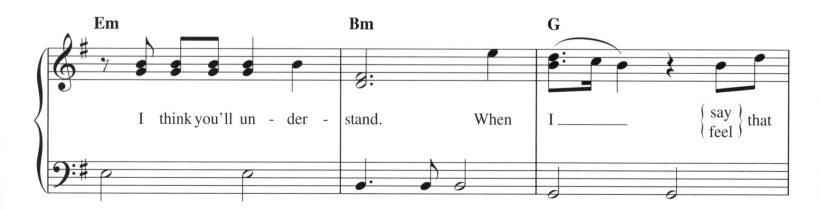

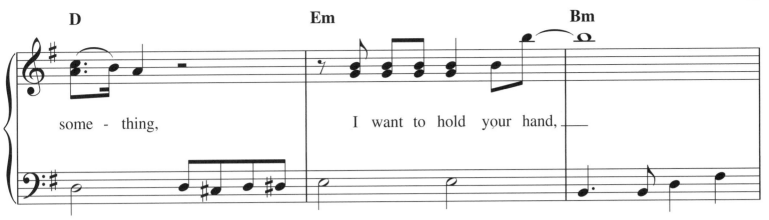

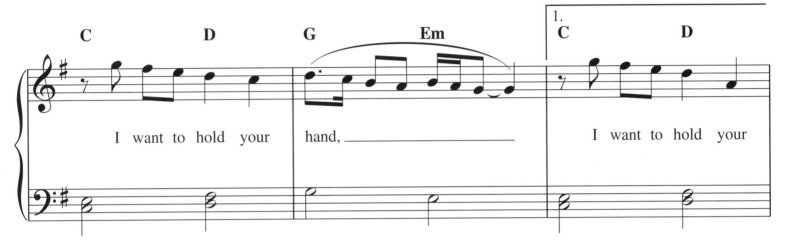

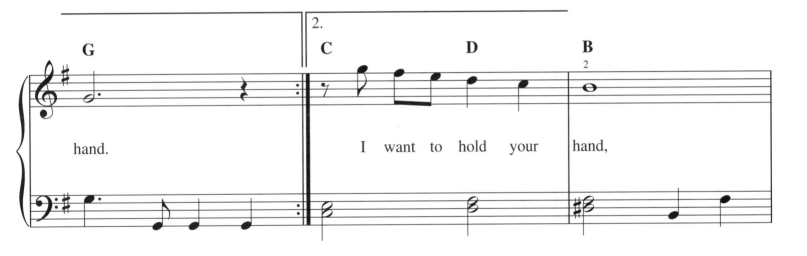

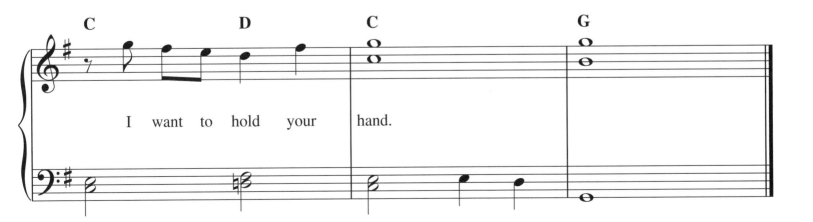

WITH A LITTLE HELP FROM MY FRIENDS

Words and Music by JOHN LENNON
and PAUL McCARTNEY

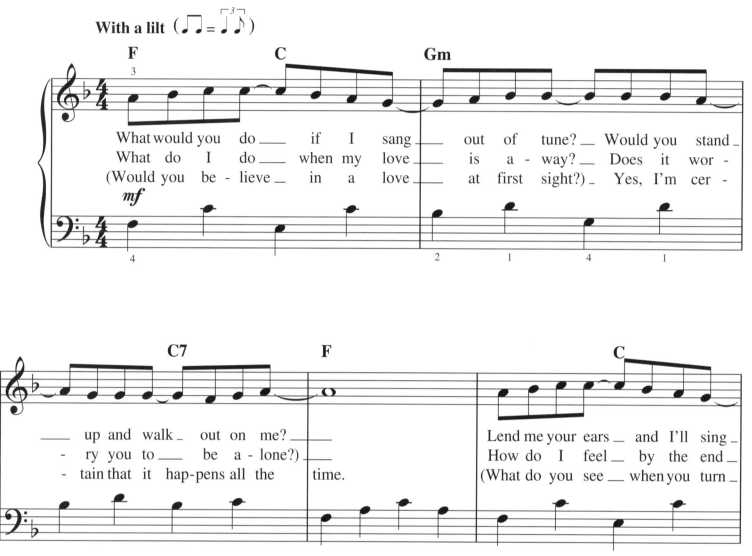

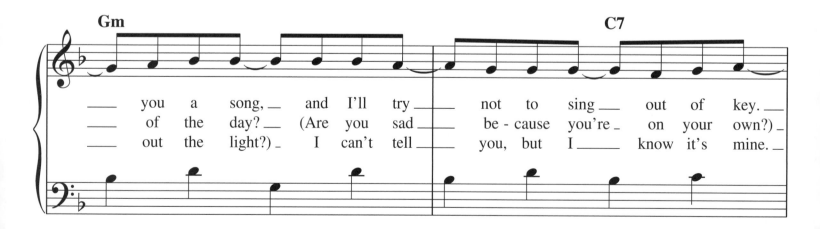

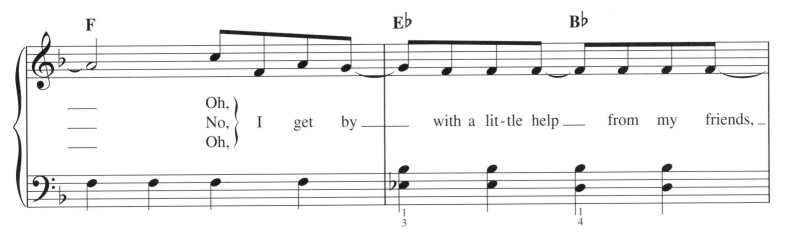

Oh,
No, } I get by ___ with a lit-tle help ___ from my friends, ___
Oh,

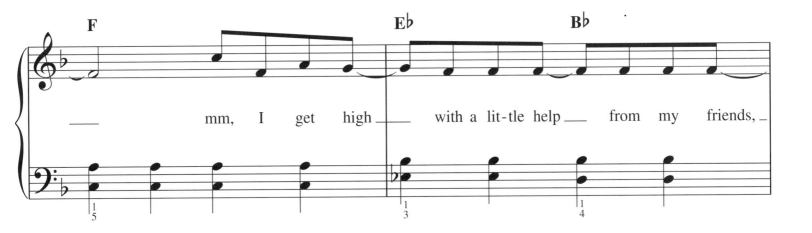

mm, I get high ___ with a lit-tle help ___ from my friends, ___

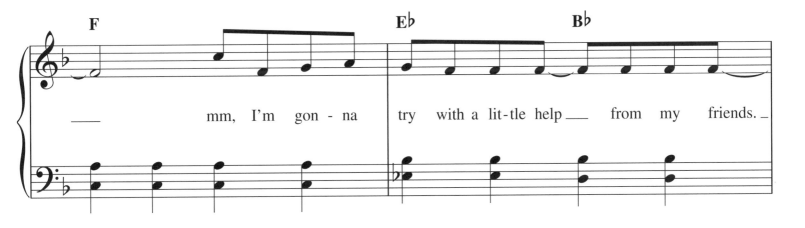

mm, I'm gon - na try with a lit-tle help ___ from my friends.

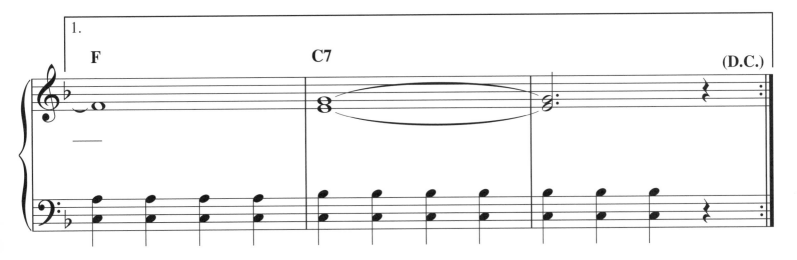

1.

(D.C.)

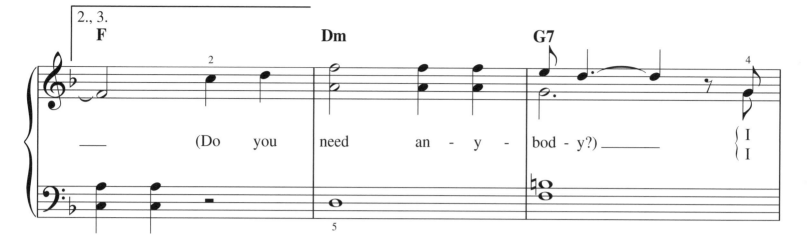

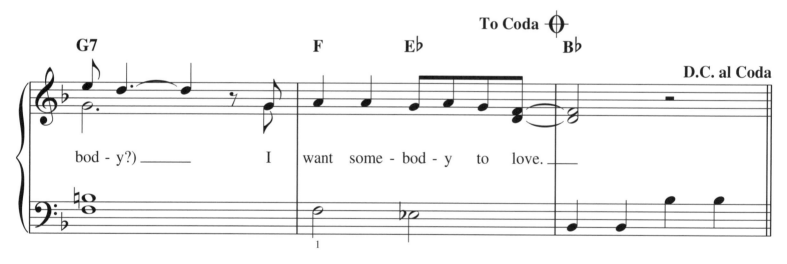

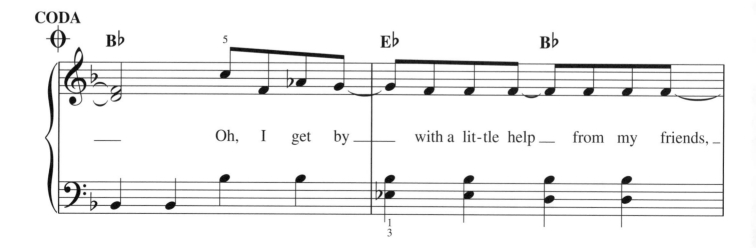

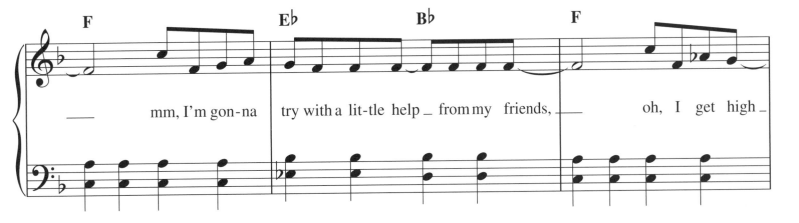

I'VE JUST SEEN A FACE

Words and Music by JOHN LENNON
and PAUL McCARTNEY

I've just seen a face, I can't for-get the time ___ or place where we just

met. She's just the girl for me, and I want all ___ the world to see we've

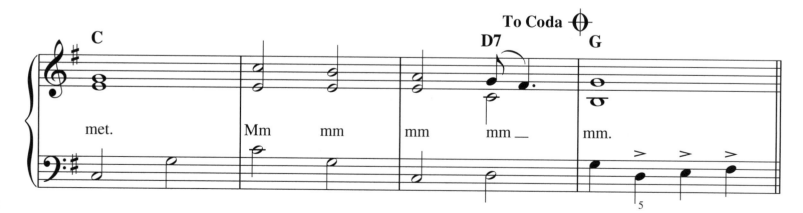

met. Mm mm mm mm ___ mm.

25

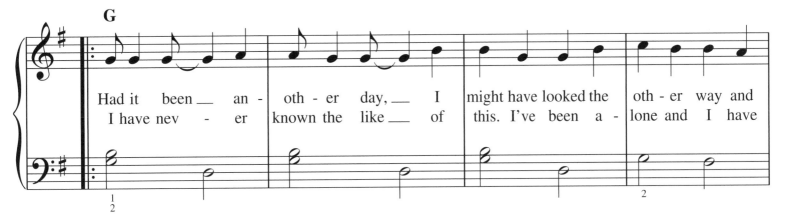

Had it been __ an - oth - er day, __ I might have looked the oth - er way and
I have nev - er known the like __ of this. I've been a - lone and I have

I'd have nev - er been a - ware. __ But, as it is, I'll dream of her to -
missed things and __ kept out of sight, __ for oth - er girls were nev - er quite like

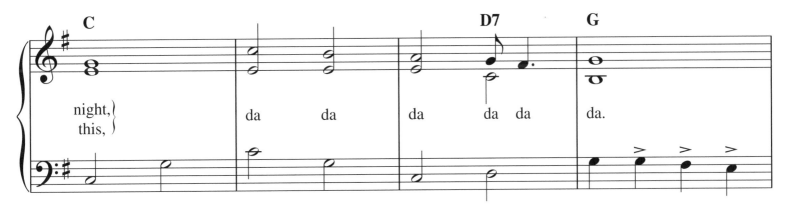

night,
this, } da da da da da da.

Fall - ing, __ yes, I am fall - ing, __ and she keeps

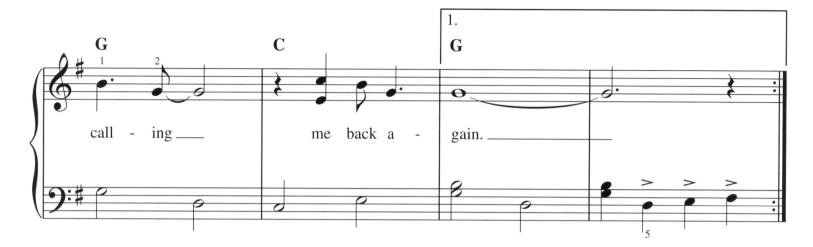

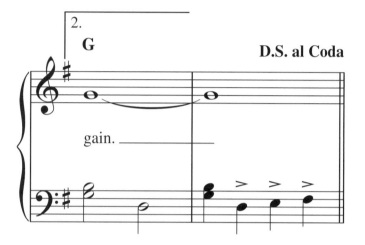

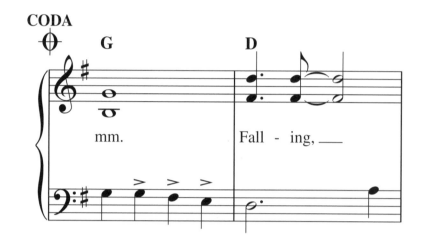

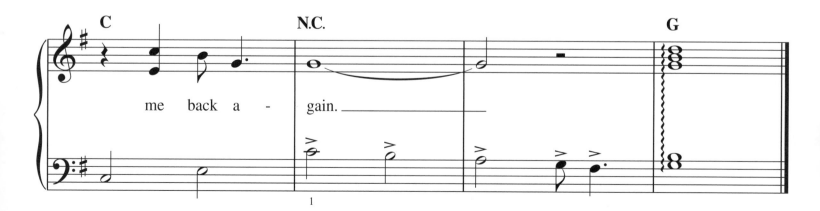

COME TOGETHER

Words and Music by JOHN LENNON
and PAUL McCARTNEY

Slow and funky

Here comes old flat-top, he come

groov-ing up slow-ly, he got   joo - joo eye-ball, he one

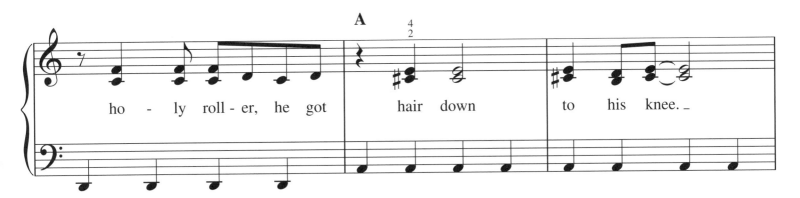

ho - ly roll-er, he got   hair down   to his knee. __

G7　　　　　　　　　　　　　　　　　　　　　　**Dm7**

Got to be a jok - er, he just　do what he　please. _

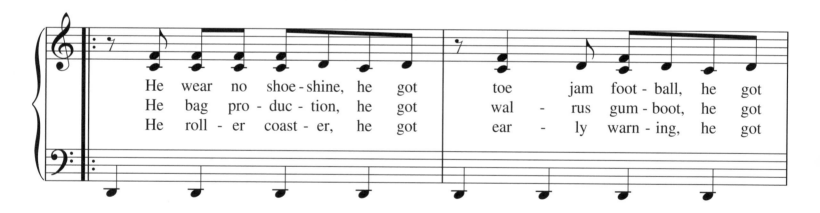

He　wear　no　shoe - shine,　he　got　　　toe　　jam　foot - ball,　he　got
He　bag　pro - duc - tion,　he　got　　　wal　-　rus　gum - boot,　he　got
He　roll - er　coast - er,　he　got　　　ear　-　ly　warn - ing,　he　got

mon　-　key　fin - ger,　he　shoot　　Co　-　ca　Co - la,　he　say,
O　-　no　side - board,　he　one　　spi　-　nal　crack - er,　he　got
Mud　-　dy　Wa - ter,　he　one　　Mo　-　jo　fil - ter,　he　say,

"I know ___ you; you know me. ___
feet down be - low ___ his knee. ___
"One and one and one ___ is three." ___

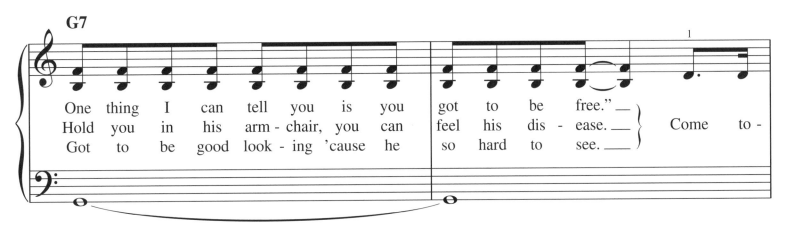

One thing I can tell you is you got to be free." ___
Hold you in his arm - chair, you can feel his dis - ease. ___ Come to -
Got to be good look - ing 'cause he so hard to see. ___

geth - er, right now, o - ver me!

1., 2.   3.   **Repeat and Fade**

DEAR PRUDENCE

Words and Music by JOHN LENNON
and PAUL McCARTNEY

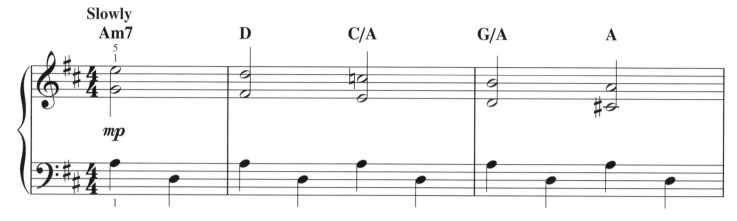

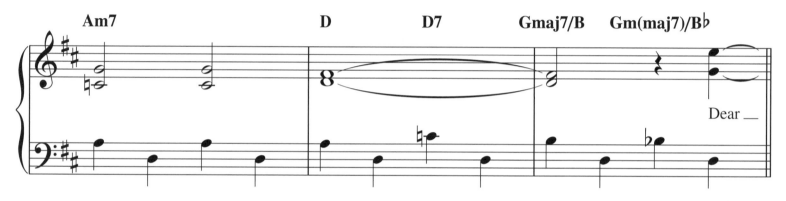

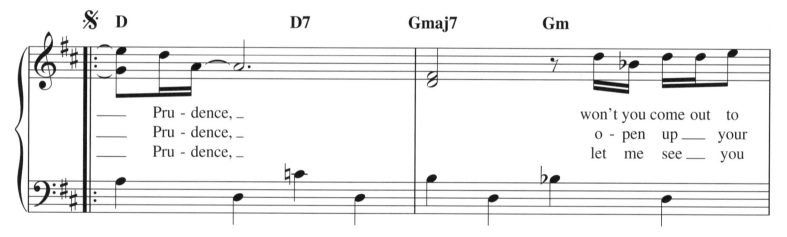

32

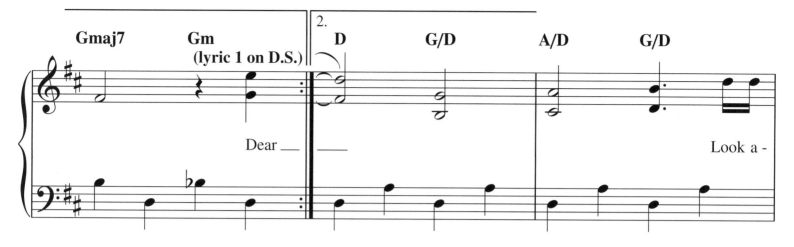

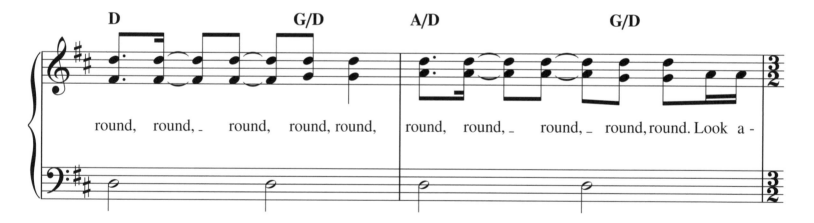

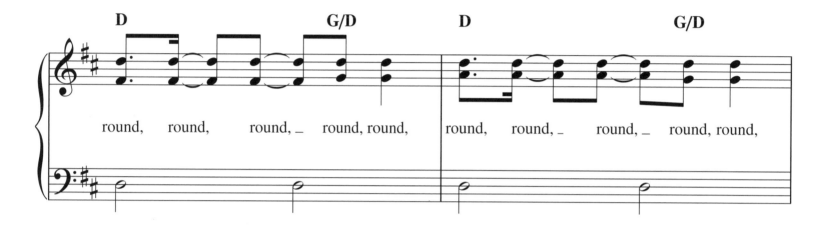

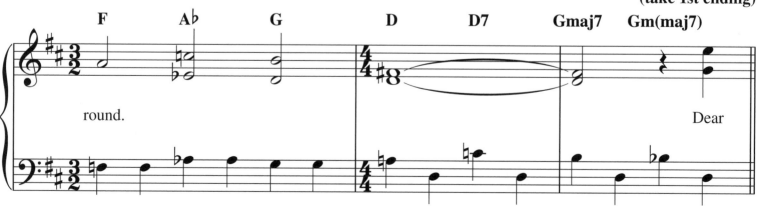

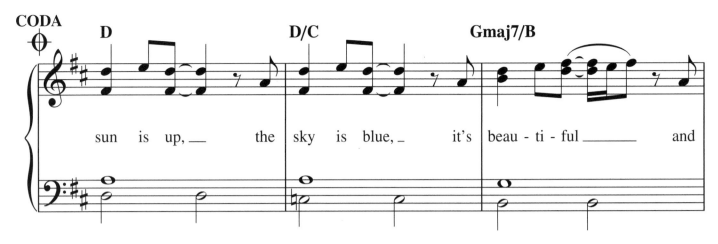

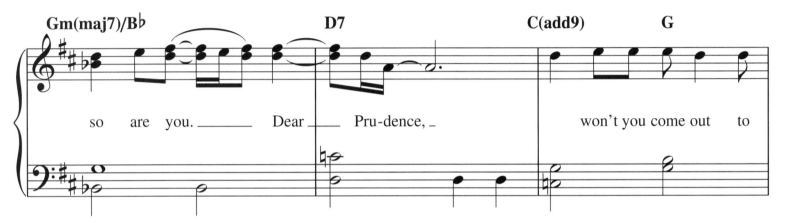

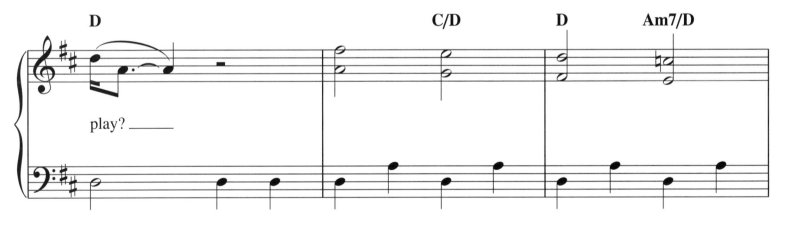

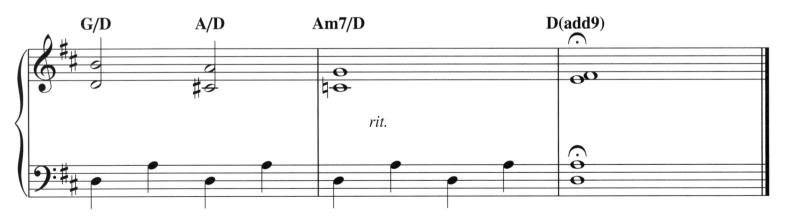

IF I FELL

Words and Music by JOHN LENNON
and PAUL McCARTNEY

Moderately slow, but not dragging

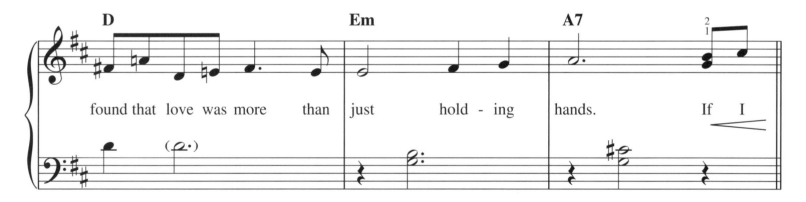

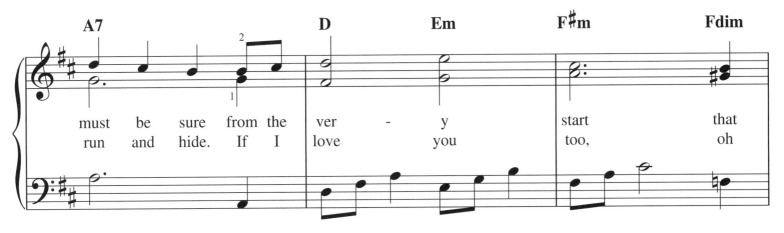

must be sure from the ver - y start that
run and hide. If I love you too, oh

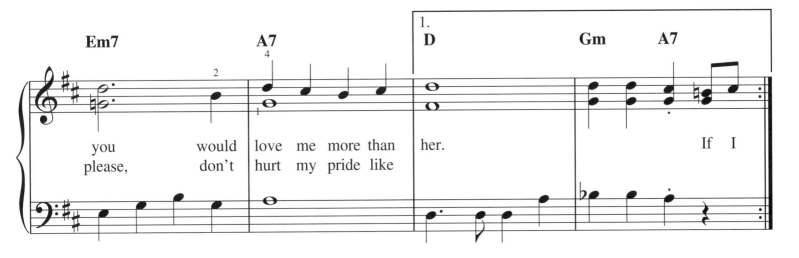

you would love me more than her.   If I
please, don't hurt my pride like

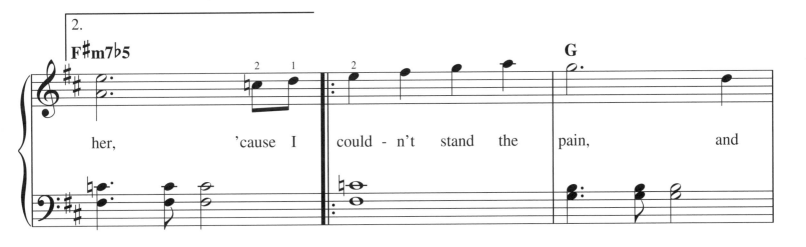

her,   'cause I could - n't stand the pain,   and

I   would be sad if our new love   was in vain. So I

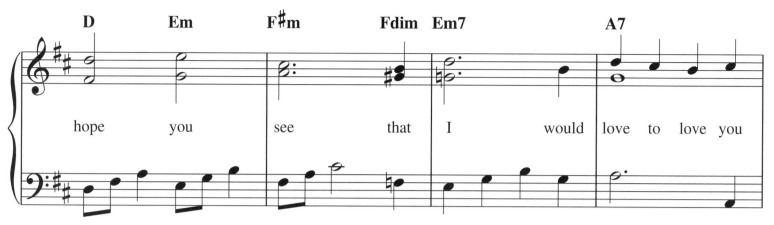

hope   you   see   that   I   would   love to love you

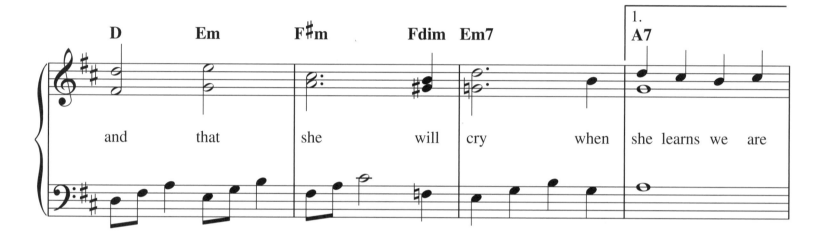

and   that   she   will   cry   when   she learns we are

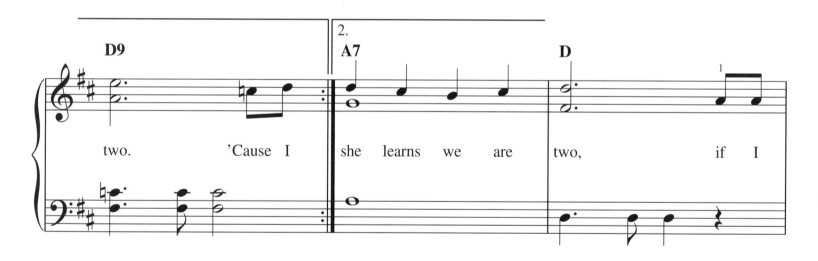

two.   'Cause I   she learns   we   are   two,   if   I

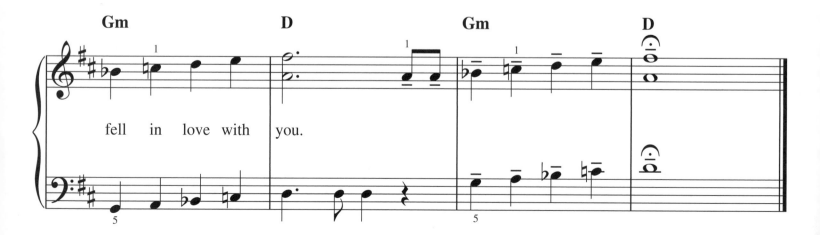

fell   in love with   you.

BLUE JAY WAY

Words and Music by
GEORGE HARRISON

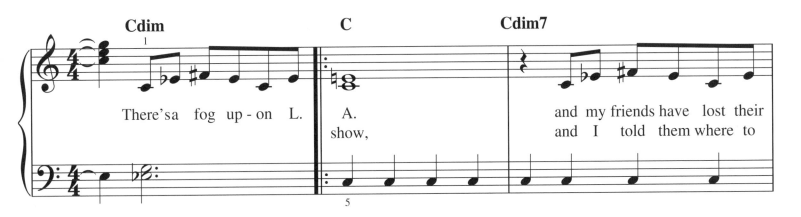

There's a fog up-on L. A.
show, and my friends have lost their
and I told them where to

way.
go. "We'll be o-ver soon," they
Ask a p'lice-man on the

said,
street, now they've lost them-selves in
there's so man-y there to

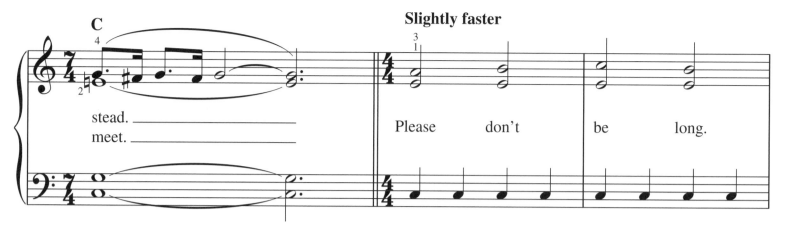

C   **Cdim**   **C**

know,   and I'd real - ly like to   go,

Cdim

soon will be the break of day,   sit-ting here in Blue Jay

C   **Slightly faster**

Way.   Please   don't

be   long,   please don't you   be ver - y long,

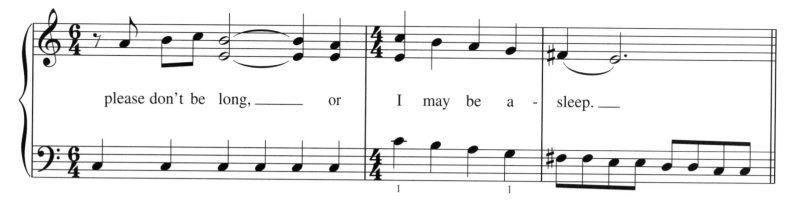

please don't be long, _____ or I may be a - sleep. __

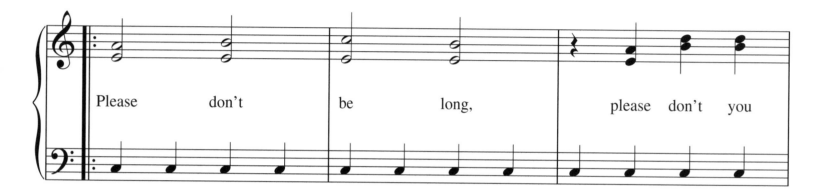

Please don't be long, please don't you

be ver - y long, please don't be long.

1., 2.

3.

please don't be long.

Don't be long, don't be long, don't be

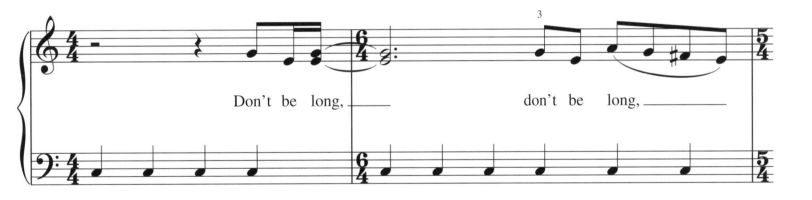

don't be long, don't be long, don't be long.

Don't be long, don't be long,

don't be long.

FLYING

Words and Music by JOHN LENNON,
PAUL McCARTNEY, GEORGE HARRISON
and RICHARD STARKEY

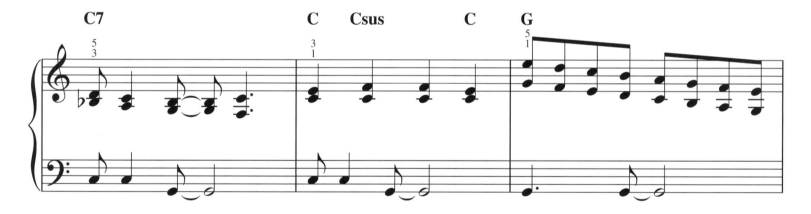

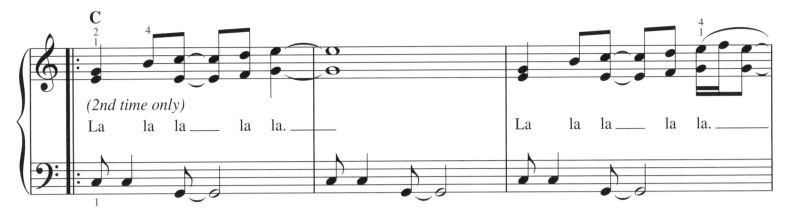

I AM THE WALRUS

Words and Music by JOHN LENNON
and PAUL McCARTNEY

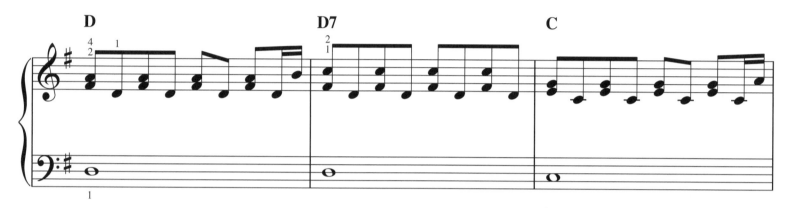

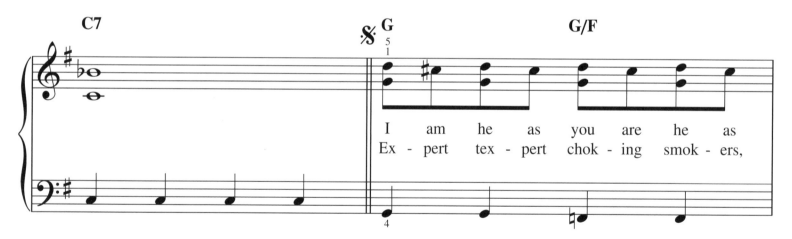

I am he as you are he as
Ex - pert tex - pert chok - ing smok - ers,

you are me and we are all to - geth - er. ____
don't you think the jok - er laughs at you? ____

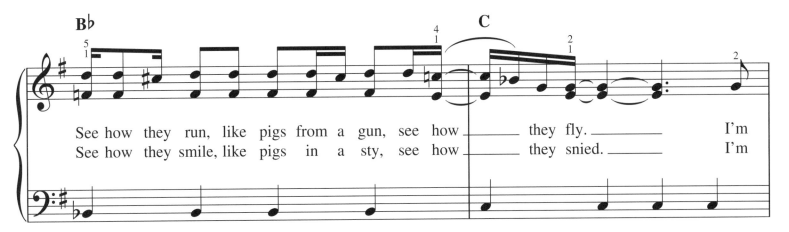

See how they run, like pigs from a gun, see how ____ they fly. ____ I'm
See how they smile, like pigs in a sty, see how ____ they snied. ____ I'm

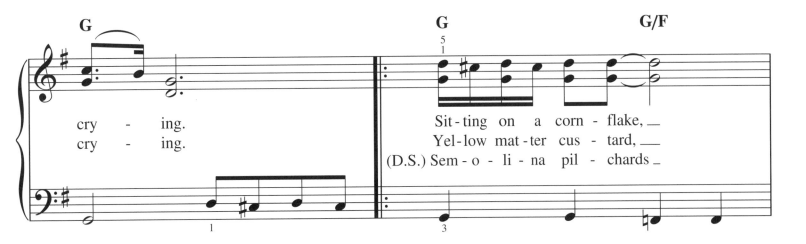

cry - ing.
cry - ing.

Sit - ting on a corn - flake, ____
Yel - low mat - ter cus - tard, ____
(D.S.) Sem - o - li - na pil - chards ____

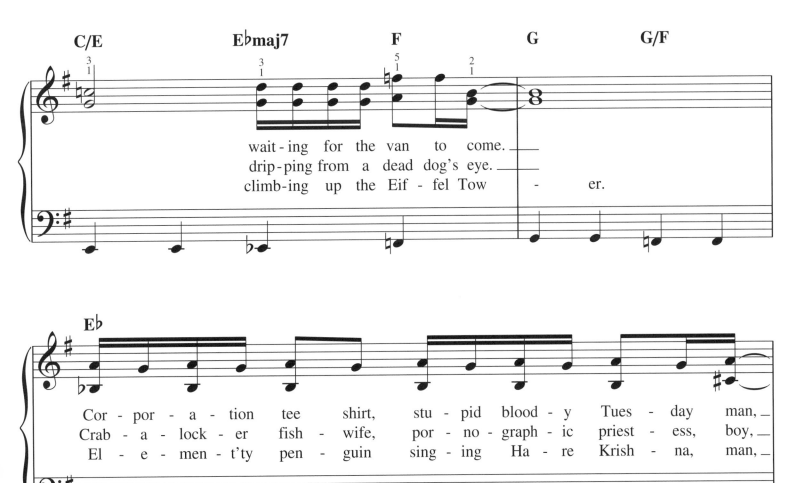

wait - ing for the van to come. ____
drip - ping from a dead dog's eye. ____
climb - ing up the Eif - fel Tow - er.

Cor - por - a - tion tee shirt, stu - pid blood - y Tues - day man, ___
Crab - a - lock - er fish - wife, por - no - graph - ic priest - ess, boy, ___
El - e - men - t'ty pen - guin sing - ing Ha - re Krish - na, man, ___

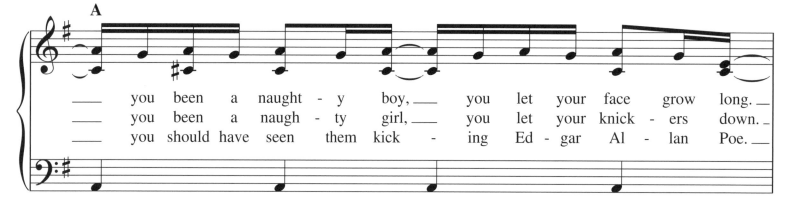

you been a naugh - ty boy, ___ you let your face grow long. ___
you been a naugh - ty girl, ___ you let your knick - ers down. ___
you should have seen them kick - ing Ed - gar Al - lan Poe. ___

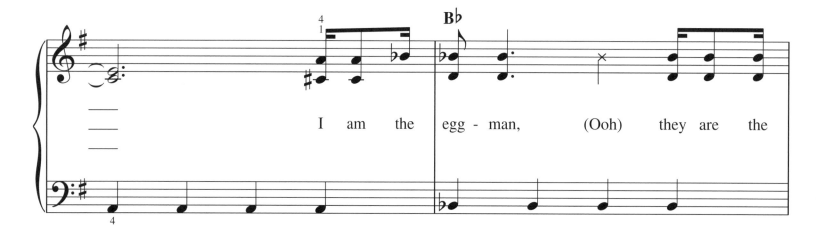

I am the egg - man, (Ooh) they are the

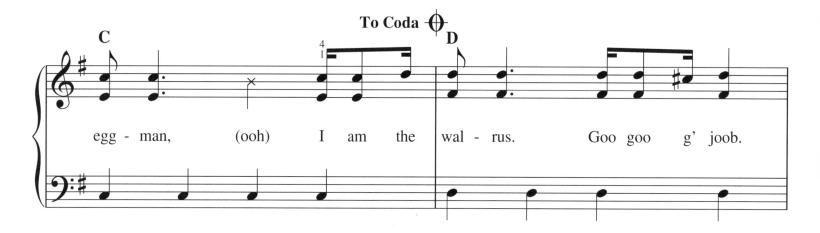

egg - man, (ooh) I am the wal - rus. Goo goo g' joob.

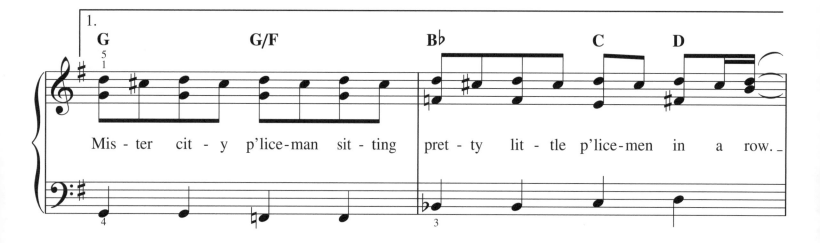

Mis - ter cit - y p'lice-man sit - ting pret - ty lit - tle p'lice-men in a row. ___

See how they fly, like Lu - cy in the sky, see how

____ they run. ____ I'm cry - ing. ____ I'm cry -

- ing. I'm cry - ing. ____ I'm cry -

ing.

Sit-ting in an En-glish gar - den wait-ing for the sun.

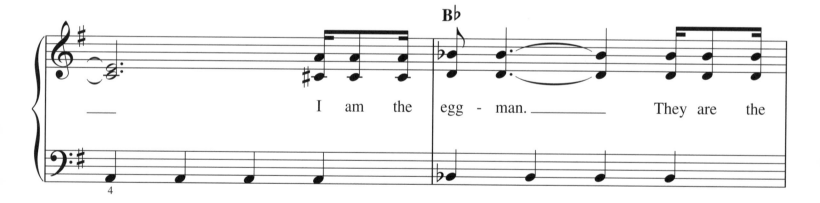

_____ If the sun don't come, ____ you get a tan from stand - ing in the En-glish rain. _

I am the egg - man. _____ They are the

egg - man. _____ I am the wal - rus. Goo goo g' joob g' goo _

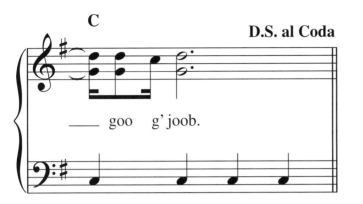

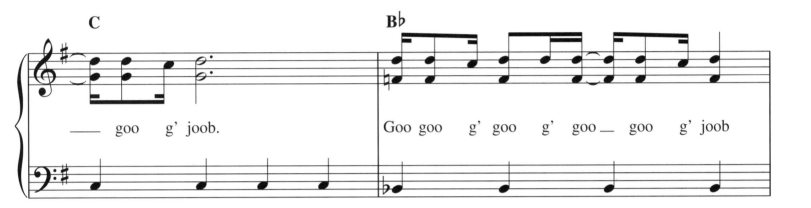

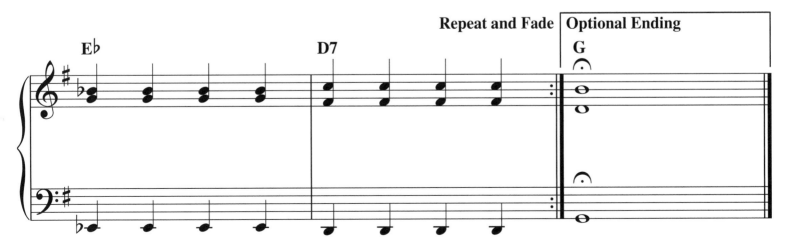

BEING FOR THE BENEFIT OF MR. KITE

Words and Music by JOHN LENNON and PAUL McCARTNEY

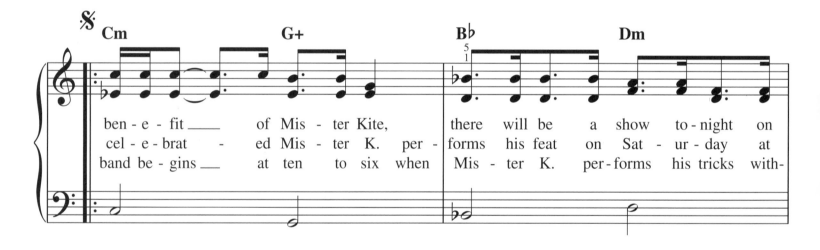

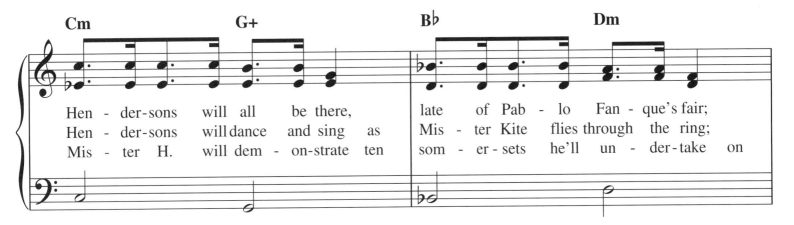

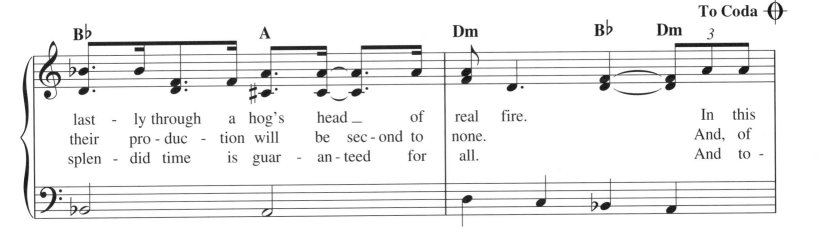

The

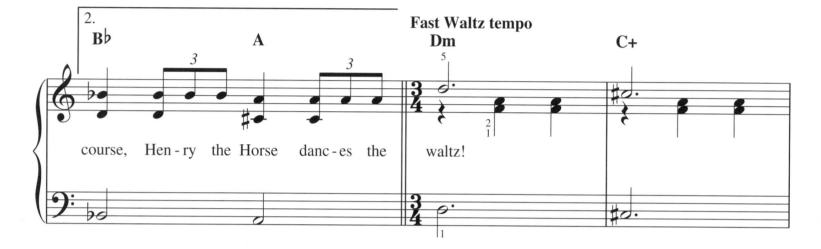

course, Hen - ry the Horse danc - es the waltz!

Fast Waltz tempo

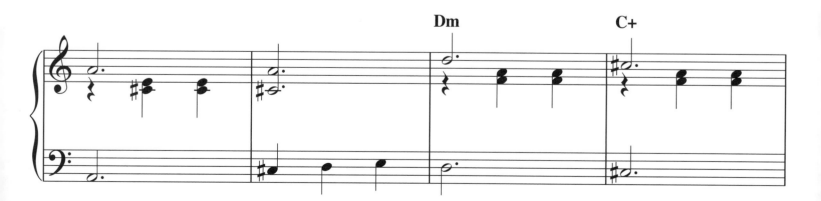

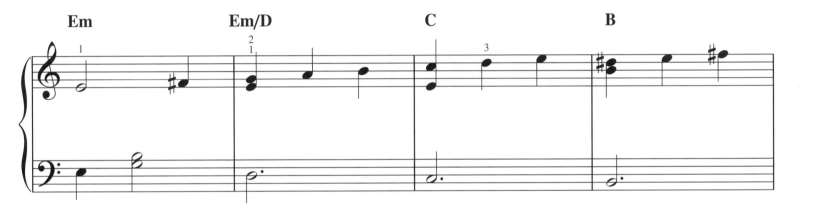

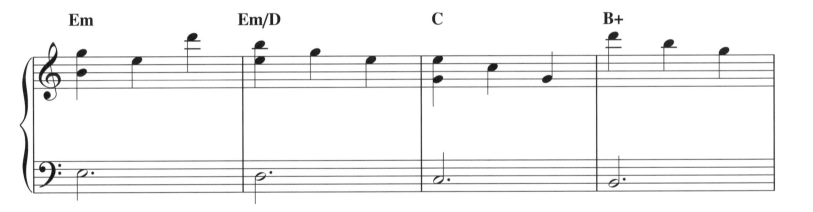

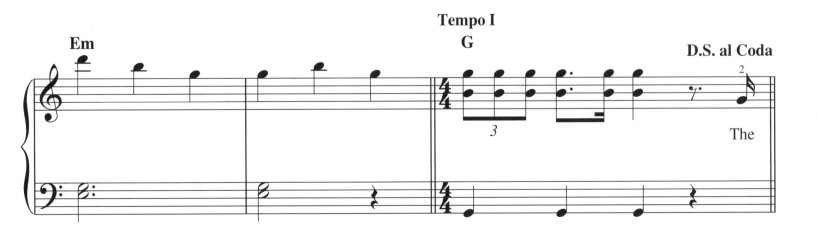

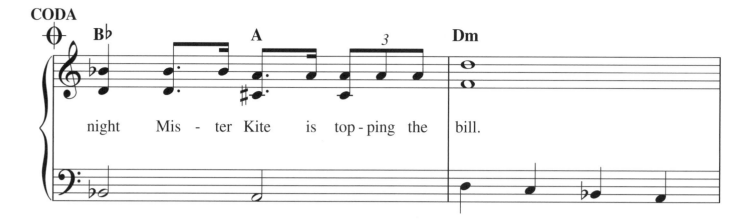

night Mis - ter Kite is top - ping the bill.

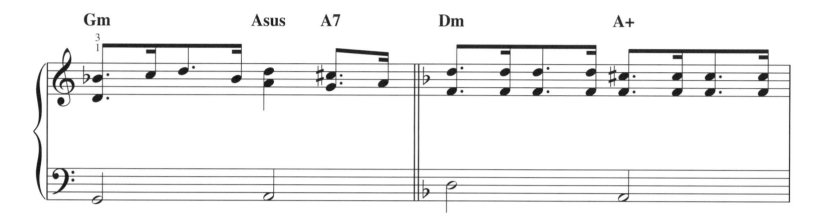

BECAUSE

Words and Music by JOHN LENNON
and PAUL MCARTNEY

Moderately slow

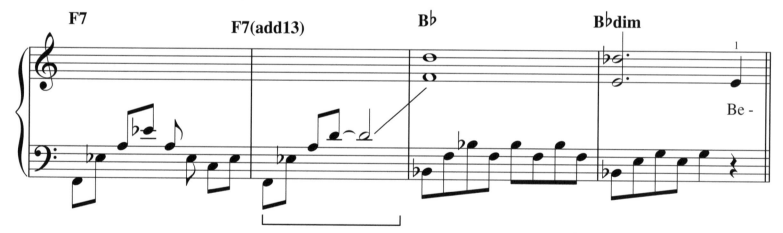

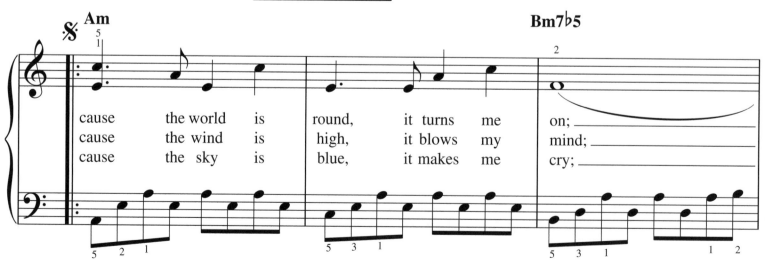

cause the world is round, it turns me on;
cause the wind is high, it blows my mind;
cause the sky is blue, it makes me cry;

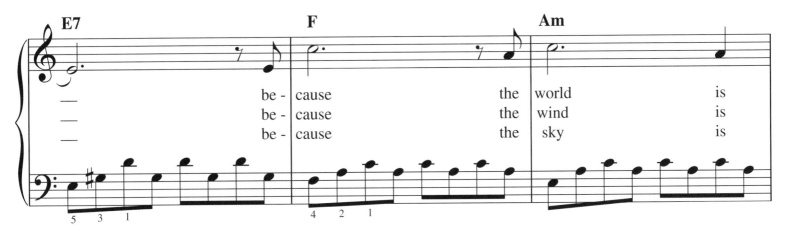

be - cause | the world | is
be - cause | the wind | is
be - cause | the sky | is

round.
high.
blue.

Ah. _____
Ah. _____

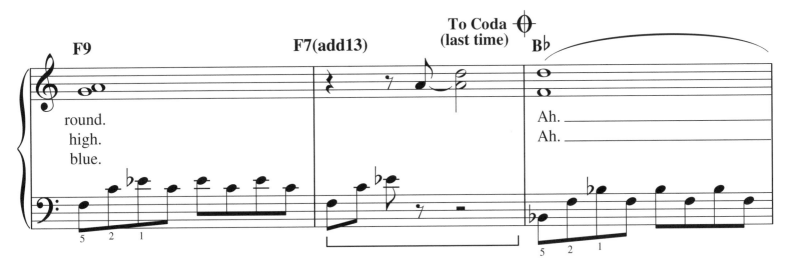

_____ | Be -

_____ Love is old, love is | new;

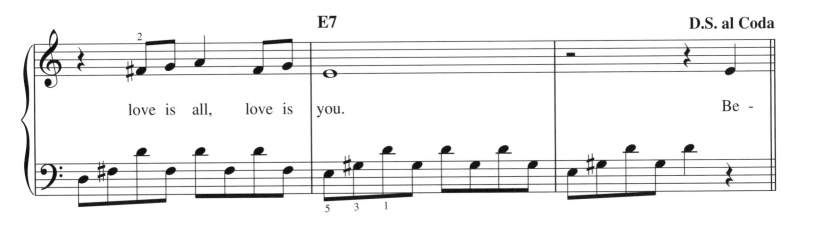

love is all,   love is | you.

Be -

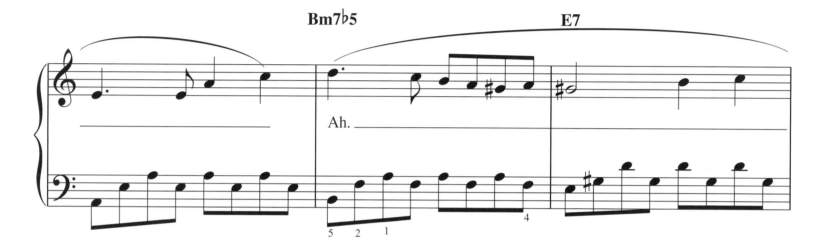

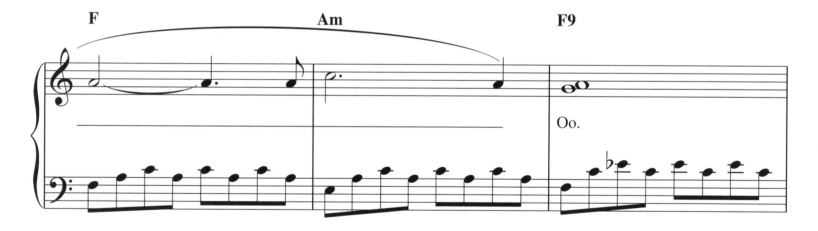

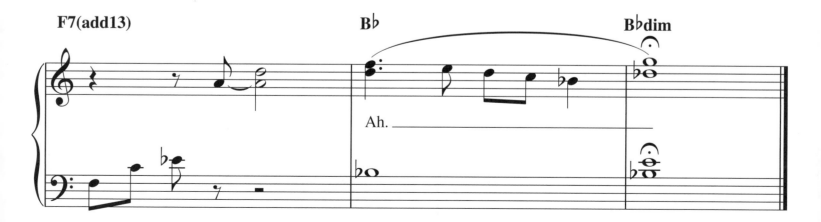

SOMETHING

Words and Music by
GEORGE HARRISON

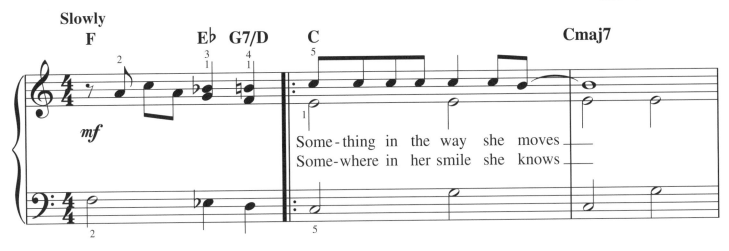

at-tracts me like no oth-er lov-er, _____ some-thing in the way she
that I don't need no oth-er lov-er, _____ some-thing in her style that

woos _ me.} I don't want to leave _ her now, you
shows _ me.}

know I be-lieve _ and how. _

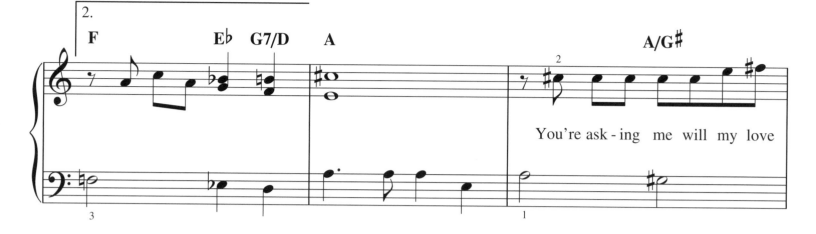

You're ask-ing me will my love

grow? I don't know, ___ I don't know.

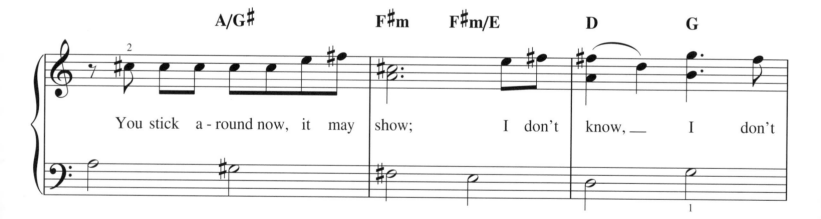

You stick a-round now, it may show; I don't know, ___ I don't

know. Some-thing in the way she knows, ___

and all I have to do is think of her, some-thing in the things she

shows _ me. I don't want to leave _ her now, you

know I be - lieve _ and how. _

WHILE MY GUITAR GENTLY WEEPS

Words and Music by
GEORGE HARRISON

Moderately

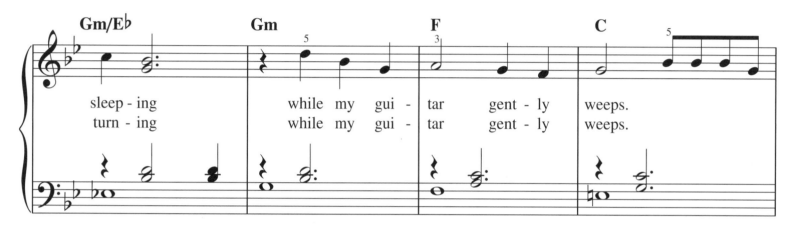

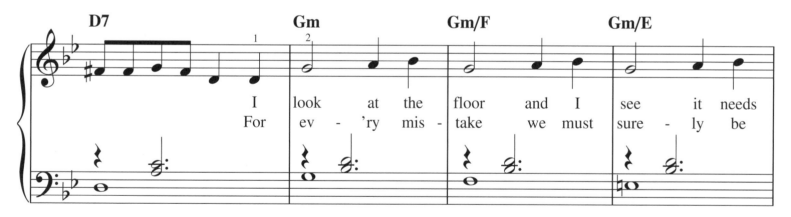

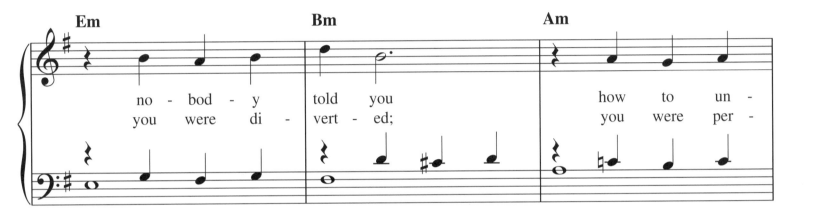

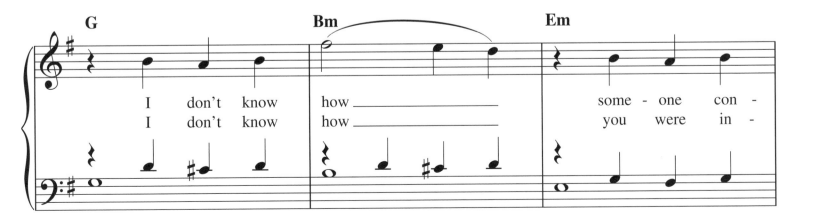

64

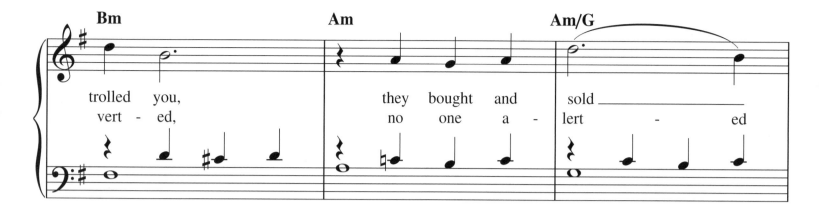

trolled you,
vert - ed,
they bought and
no one a -
sold ⎯⎯⎯
lert - ed

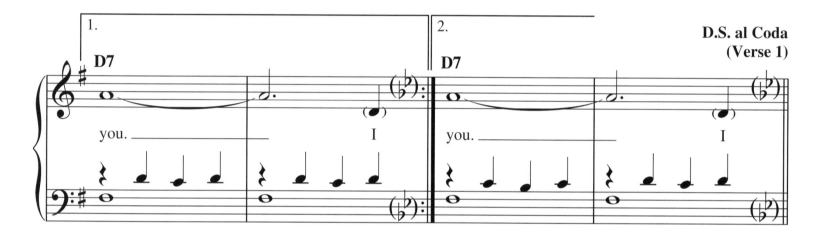

you. ⎯⎯ I
you. ⎯⎯ I

D.S. al Coda
(Verse 1)

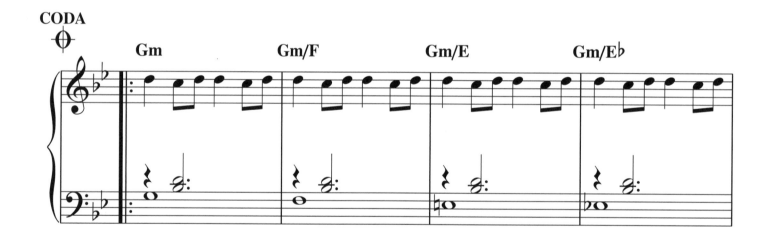

CODA

Gm **Gm/F** **Gm/E** **Gm/E♭**

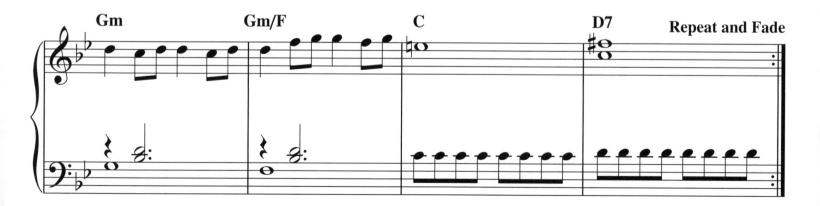

Gm **Gm/F** **C** **D7** **Repeat and Fade**

REVOLUTION

Words and Music by JOHN LENNON
and PAUL McCARTNEY

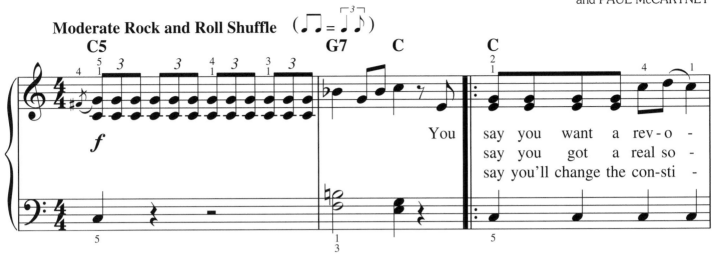

You
say you want a rev-o -
say you got a real so -
say you'll change the con-sti -

lu - tion; _____ well, _____ you know, _____ we all
lu - tion; _____ well, _____ you know, _____ we'd all
tu - tion; _____ well, _____ you know, _____ we all

want to change the world.
love to see the plan.
want to change your head.

You
You
You

tell me that it's e - vo - lu - tion; _____ well, _____ you know,
ask me for a con - tri - bu - tion; _____ well, _____ you know,
tell me it's the in - sti - tu - tion; _____ well, _____ you know,

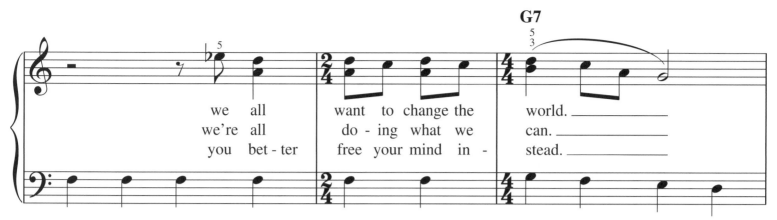

we all / we're all / you bet-ter — want to change the / do-ing what we / free your mind in- — world. / can. / stead.

But when you talk a-bout de- / But if you want mon-ey for peo-ple with / But if you go car-ry-ing pic-tures of

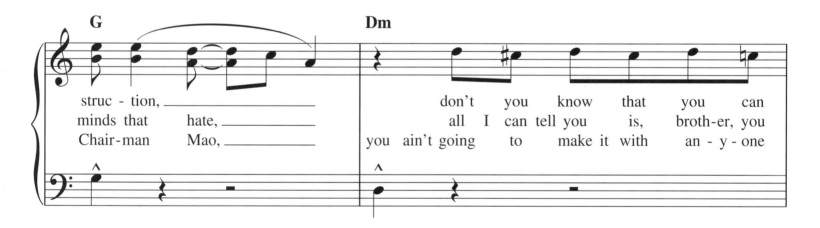

struc-tion, / minds that hate, / Chair-man Mao, — don't you know that you can / all I can tell you is, broth-er, you / you ain't going to make it with an-y-one

count me out? / have to wait. / an-y-how. — Don't you know it's gon-na be al-

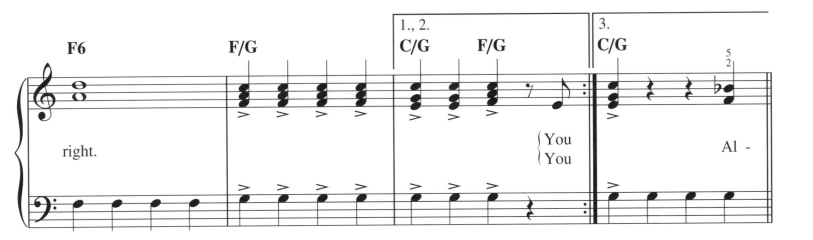

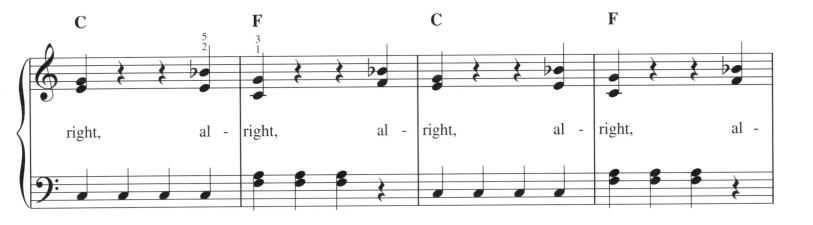

OH! DARLING

Words and Music by JOHN LENNON
and PAUL McCARTNEY

Slowly, in 2

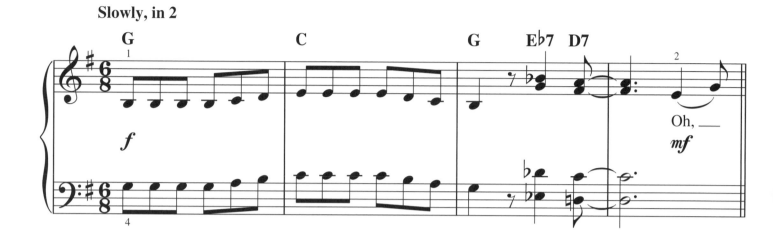

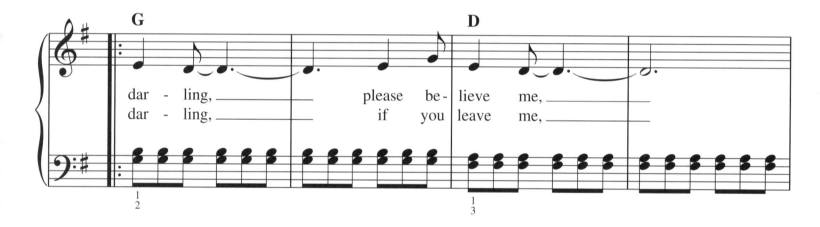

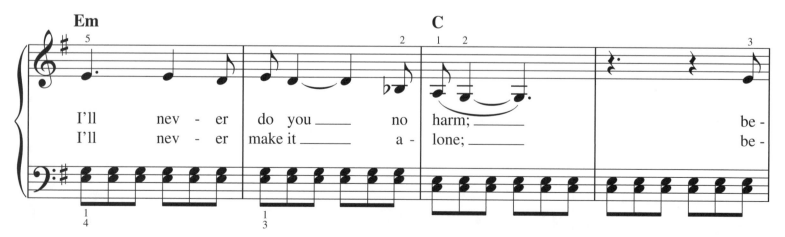

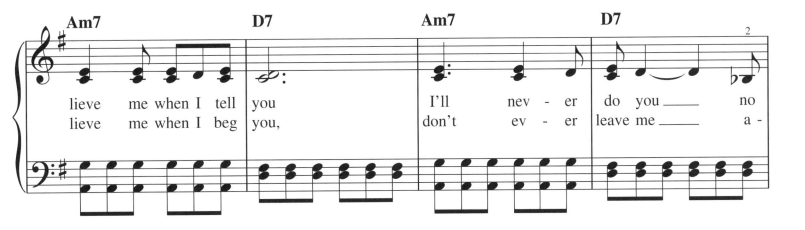

lieve   me when I tell you   I'll   nev - er   do you ___ no
lieve   me when I beg you,   don't   ev - er   leave me ___ a -

harm. ___   Oh, ___
lone. ___

When you   told   me _____   you did-n't

need   me an - y - more, ___ well, you know   I near - ly   broke down ___ and

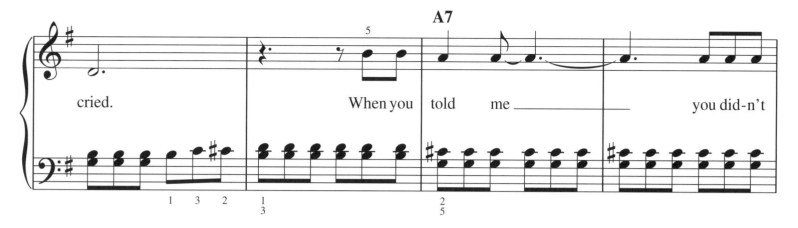

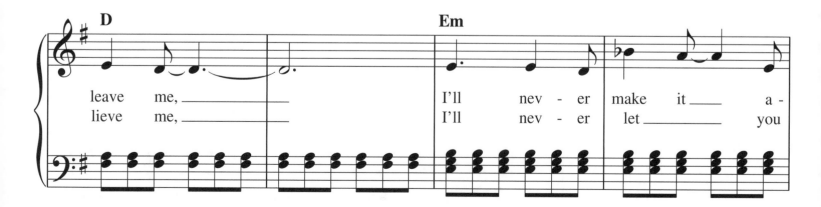

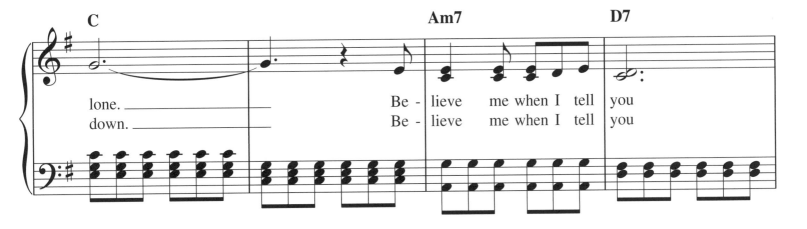

STRAWBERRY FIELDS FOREVER

Words and Music by JOHN LENNON
and PAUL McCARTNEY

Slowly, but not dragging

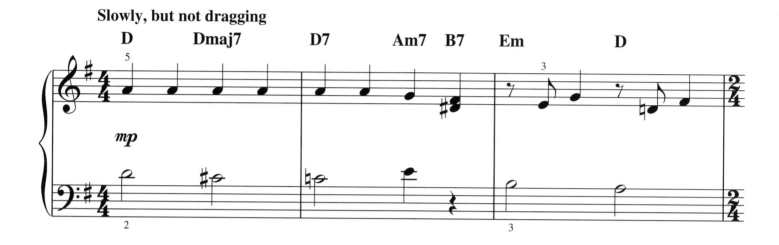

Let me take you down 'cause I'm go - in'

to Straw - ber - ry Fields. Noth - ing is

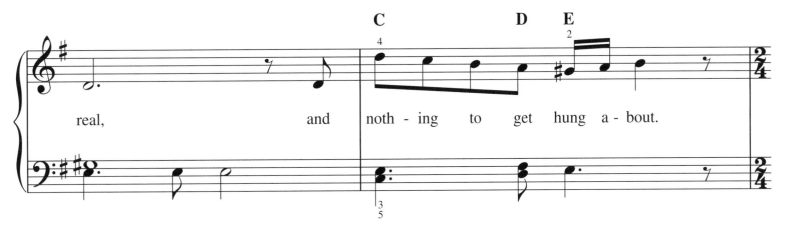

real, and noth - ing to get hung a - bout.

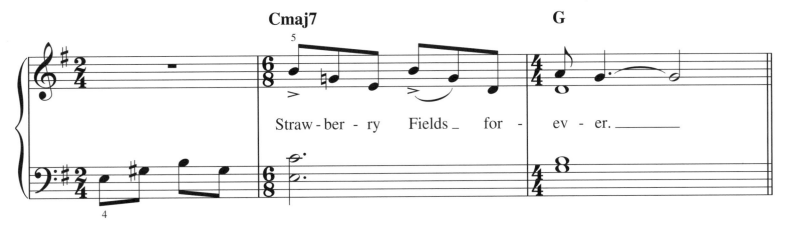

Straw - ber - ry Fields __ for - ev - er. _____

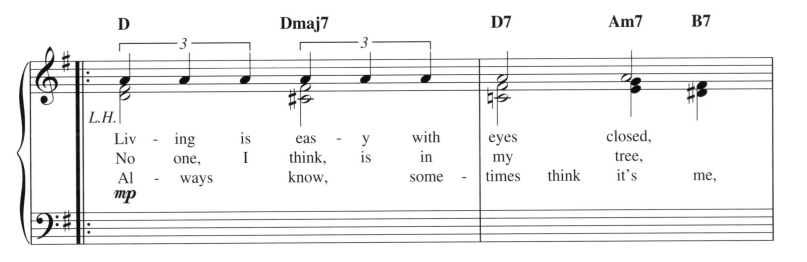

Liv - ing is eas - y with eyes closed,
No one, I think, is in my tree,
Al - ways know, some - times think it's me,

mp

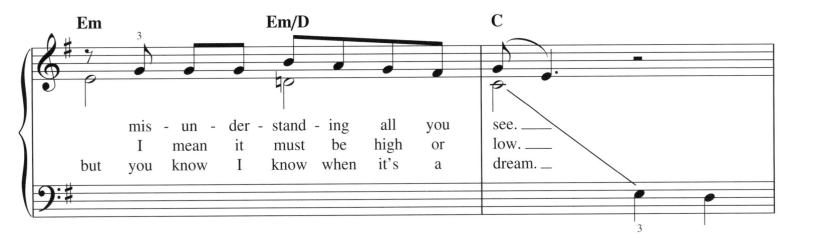

mis - un - der - stand - ing all you see. ____
I mean it must be high or low. ____
but you know I know when it's a dream. __

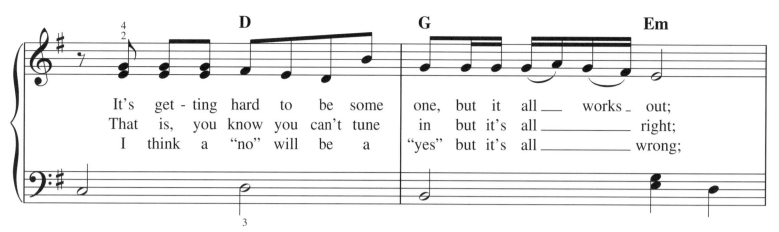

D   **G**   **Em**

It's get - ting hard to be some | one, but it all ___ works _ out;
That is, you know you can't tune | in but it's all _____ right;
I think a "no" will be a | "yes" but it's all _____ wrong;

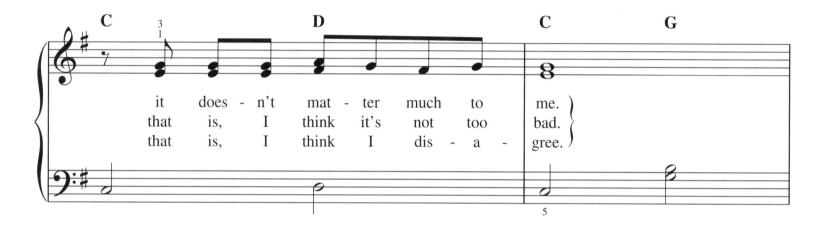

C   **D**   **C**   **G**

it does - n't mat - ter much to | me.
that is, I think it's not too | bad.
that is, I think I dis - a - | gree.

Dm7

mf Let me take you | down 'cause I'm go - in' | to Straw - ber - ry

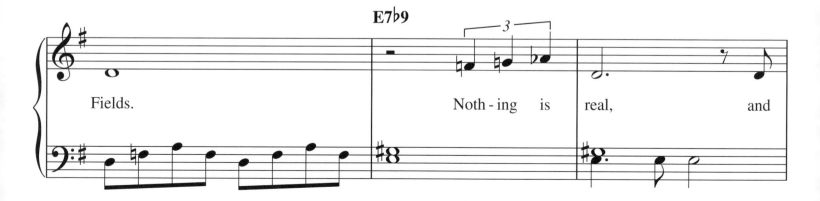

E7♭9

Fields. | Noth - ing is real, | and

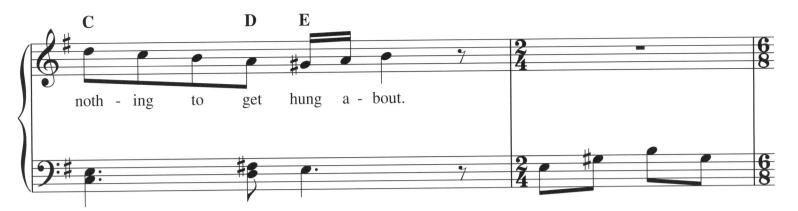

noth - ing to get hung a - bout.

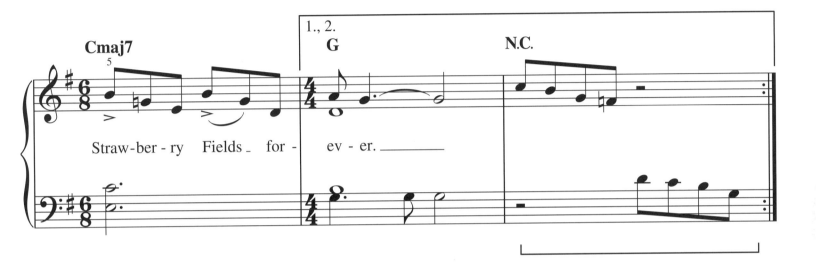

Straw - ber - ry Fields for - ev - er. _____

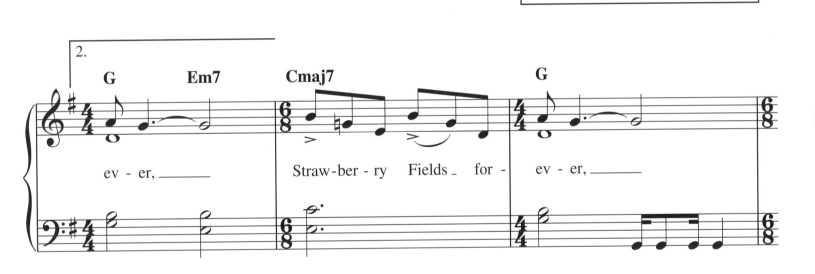

ev - er, _____ Straw - ber - ry Fields for - ev - er, _____

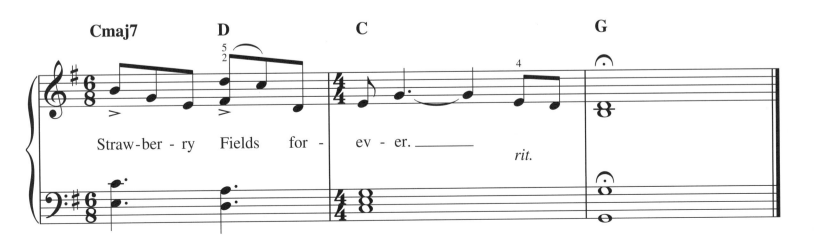

Straw - ber - ry Fields for - ev - er. _____ *rit.*

ACROSS THE UNIVERSE

Words and Music by JOHN LENNON
and PAUL McCARTNEY

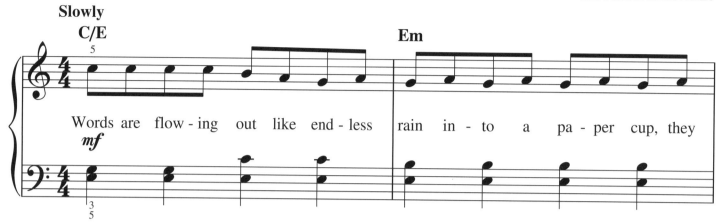

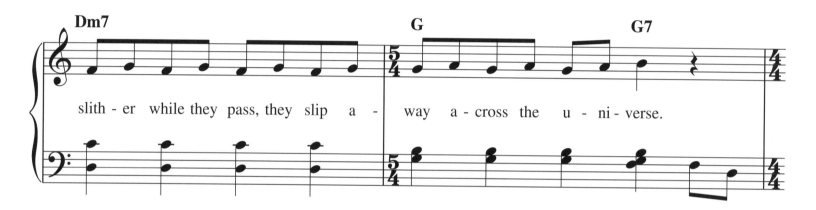

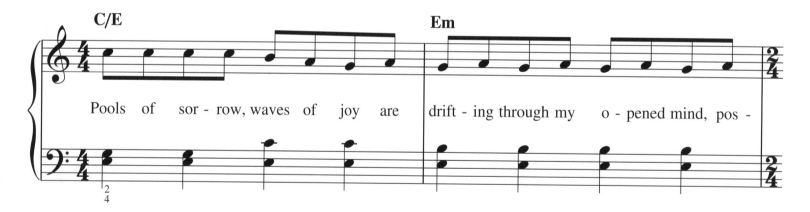

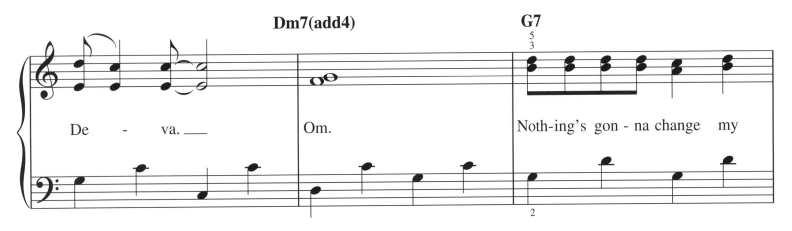

De - va. ___ Om. Noth-ing's gon - na change my

world. Noth-ing's gon - na change my world.

Noth-ing's gon - na change my world. Noth-ing's gon - na change my

To Coda ⊕

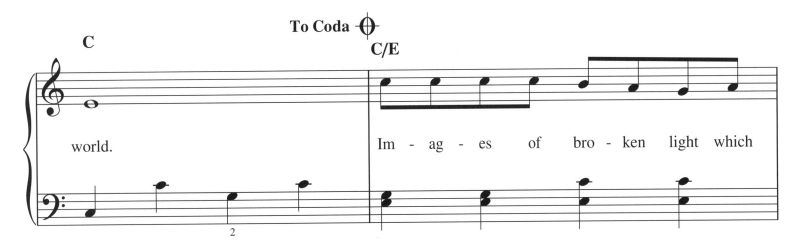

world. Im - ag - es of bro - ken light which

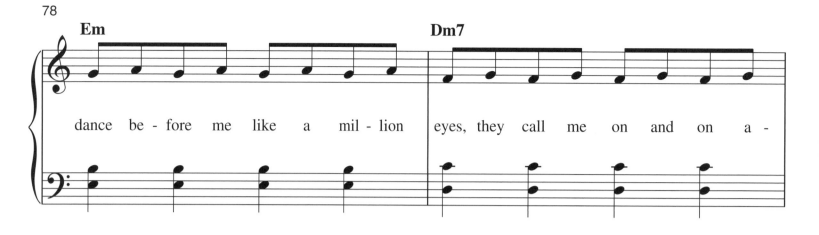

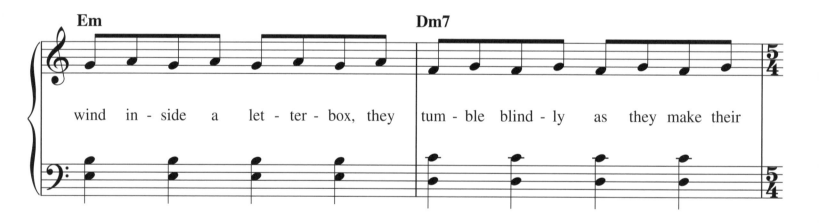

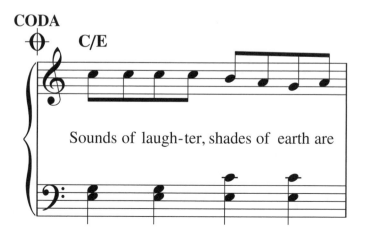

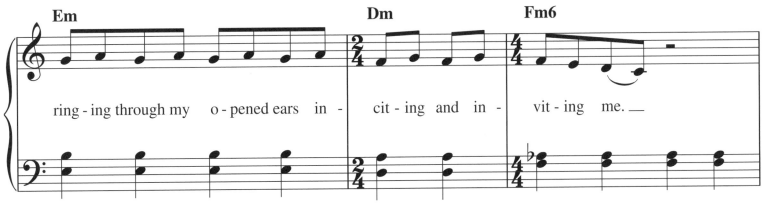

ring - ing through my o - pened ears in - cit - ing and in - vit - ing me. __

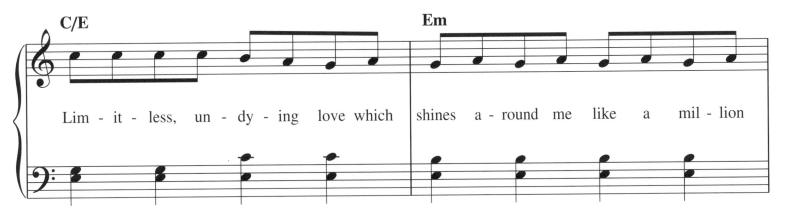

Lim - it - less, un - dy - ing love which shines a - round me like a mil - lion

suns and calls me on and on a - cross the u - ni - verse.

Repeat and Fade | **Optional Ending**

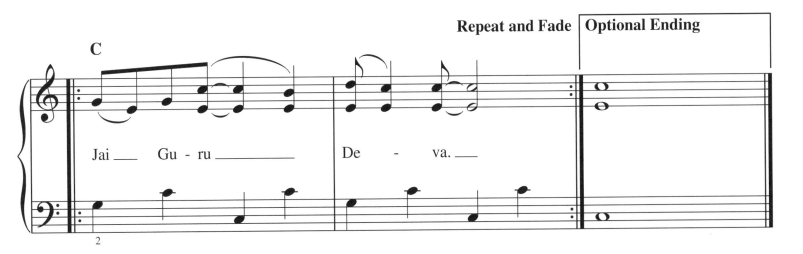

Jai __ Gu - ru __ De - va. __

HELTER SKELTER

Words and Music by JOHN LENNON
and PAUL McCARTNEY

Moderate Rock

When I

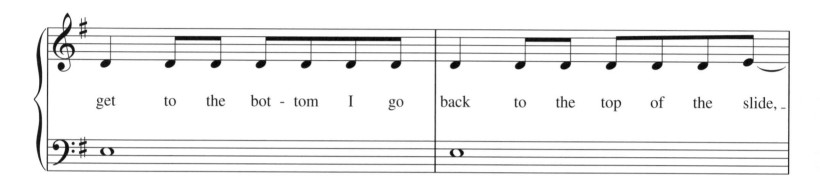

get   to the bot - tom I go   back   to the top of the slide, __

__ where I stop and I   turn   and I go for a ride, __

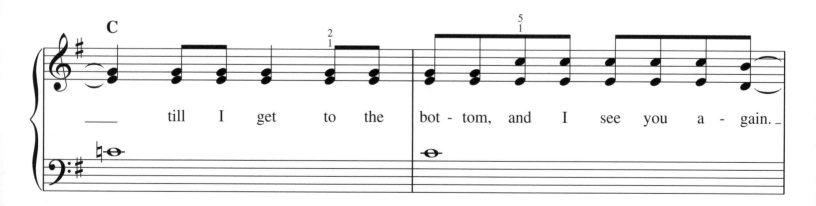

__ till I get to the   bot - tom, and I see you a - gain. __

Yeah, yeah, yeah, ___ yeah!

But do you, don't you want ___ me to love ___ you?

I'm com - ing down fast, but I'm

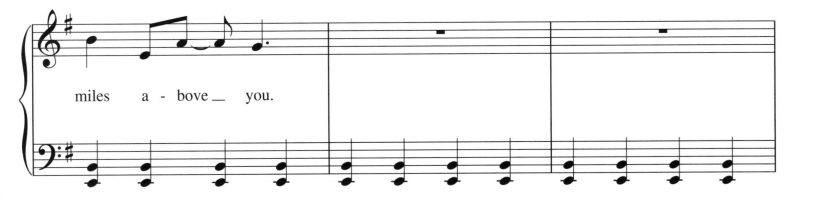

miles a - bove ___ you.

Tell me, tell me, tell ___ me, come on, tell ___ me the an - swer. ___

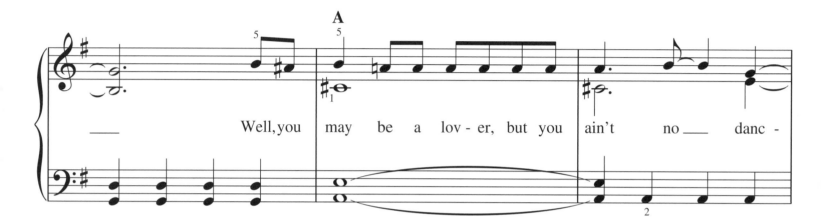

Well, you may be a lov - er, but you ain't no ___ danc -

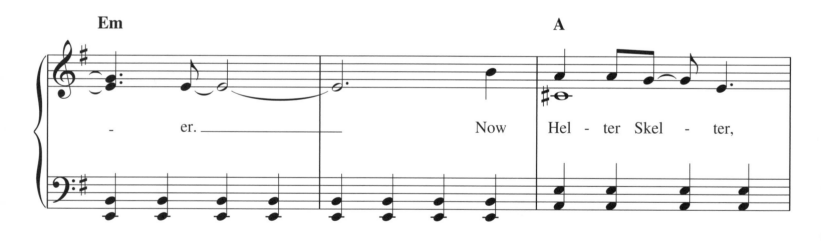

- er. _____ Now Hel - ter Skel - ter,

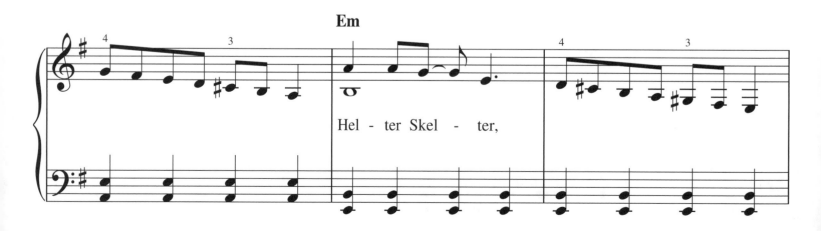

Hel - ter Skel - ter,

Hel - ter Skel - ter,   yeah,   yeah! _____

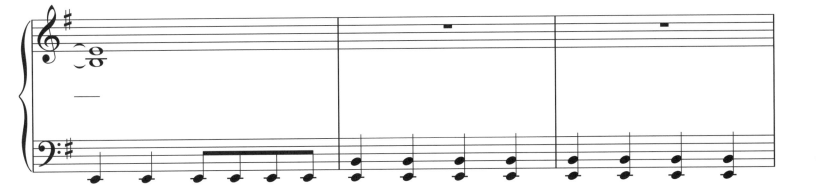

Well, will you, won't you want _____
do you, don't you want _____

_____ me to make _ you?   I'm
_____ me to make _ you?

coming down fast, but don't let me break_ you.

Tell me, tell me, tell ___ me ___ the an - swer. You

may be a lov - er, but you ain't no danc - er.

Look out! ___ Hel - ter Skel - ter,

Hel - ter Skel - ter.   Hel - ter Skel - ter,

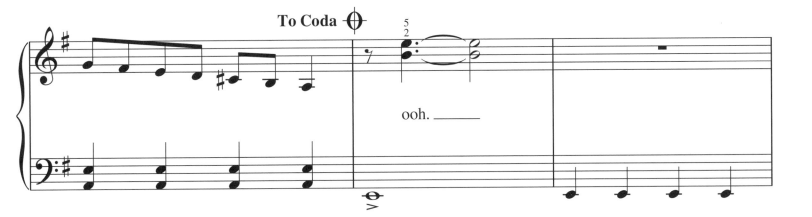

To Coda ⊕

ooh. _____

Look out!   'Cause here she   comes!

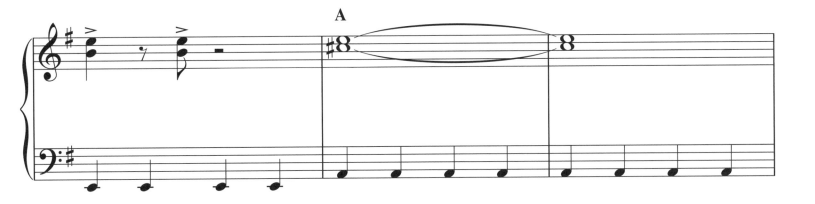

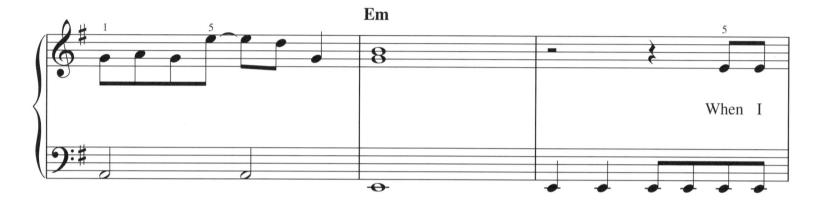

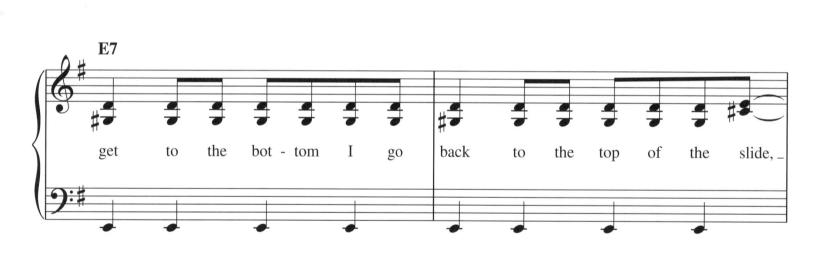

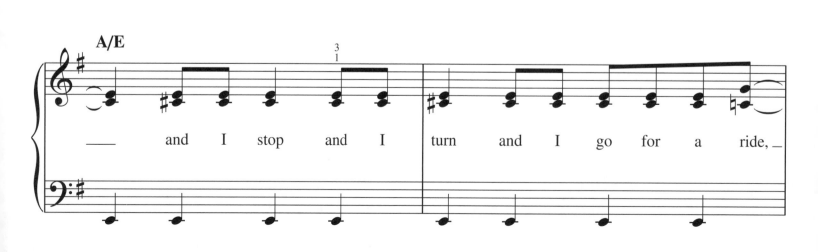

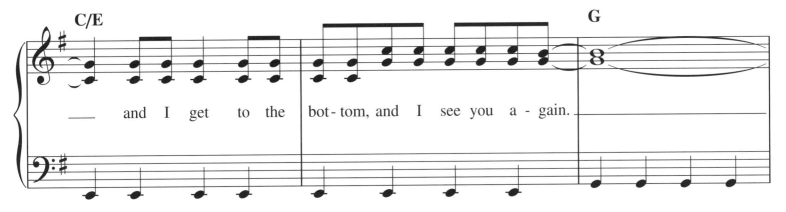

and I get to the bot-tom, and I see you a-gain.

Yeah, yeah, yeah, yeah!

Well,

(Shout, ad lib:) Look out!

Helter Skelter.

She's coming down fast!

Yes, she is. (etc.)

HAPPINESS IS A WARM GUN

Words and Music by JOHN LENNON
and PAUL McCARTNEY

Very slowly

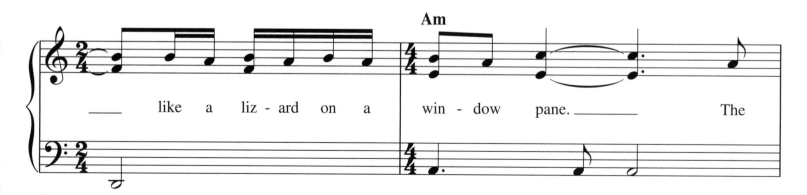

man in the crowd with the mul - ti - col - ored mir - rors on his

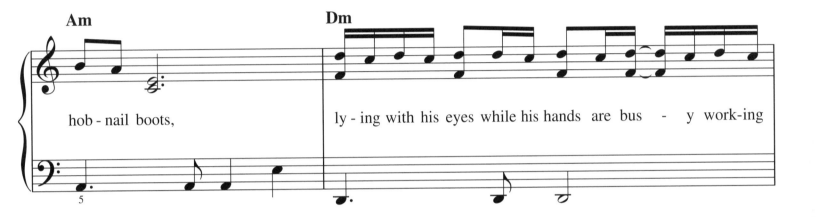

hob - nail boots,   ly - ing with his eyes while his hands are bus - y work-ing

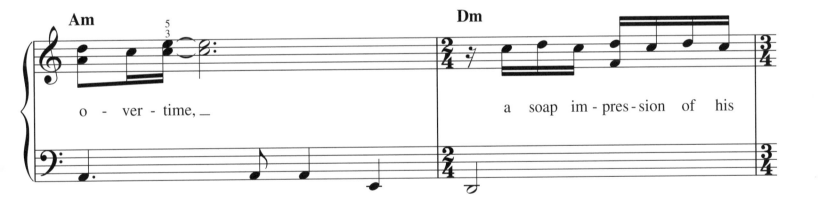

o - ver - time, _   a soap im - pres - sion of his

wife which he ate and do - nat - ed to the   Na - tion - al Trust. _

Double tempo

I need a

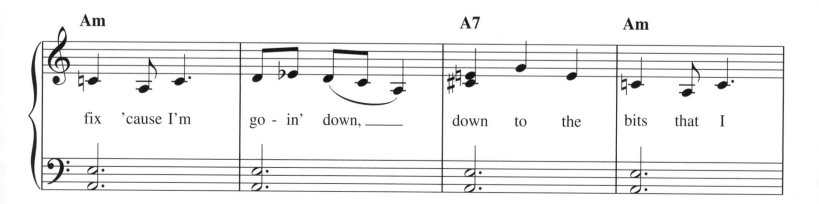

fix 'cause I'm   go - in' down, _____   down to the   bits that I

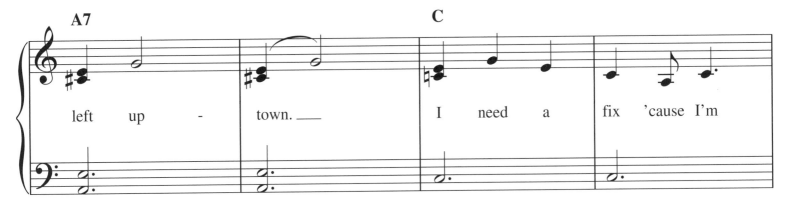

left up - town. ___ I need a fix 'cause I'm

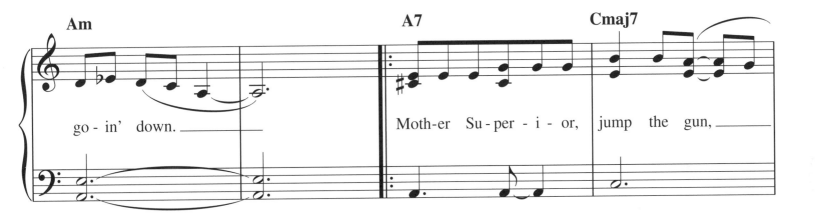

go - in' down. ___ Moth-er Su-per-i-or, jump the gun, ___

Moth er Su-per-i-or jump the gun. ___

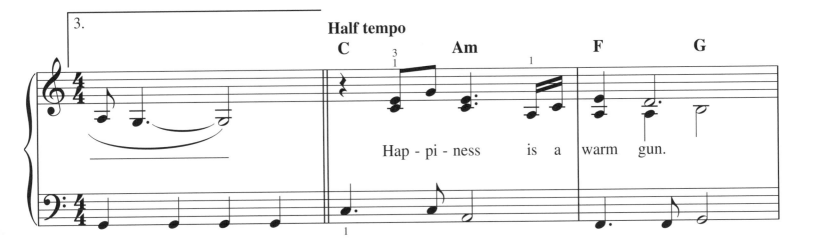

Hap - pi - ness is a warm gun.

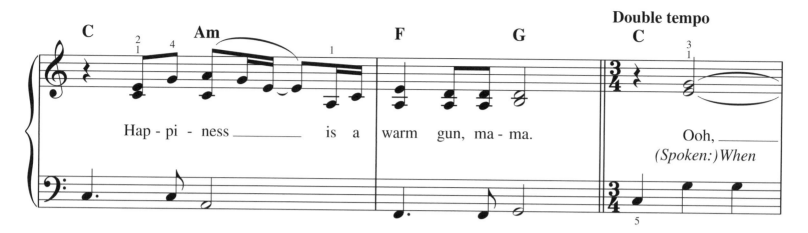

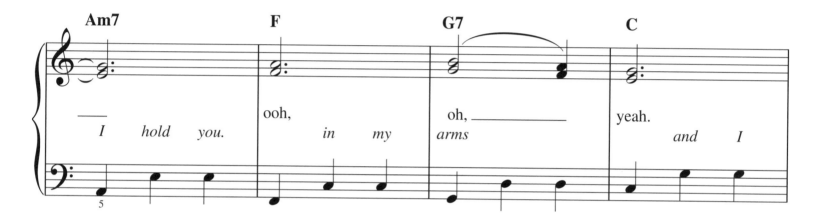

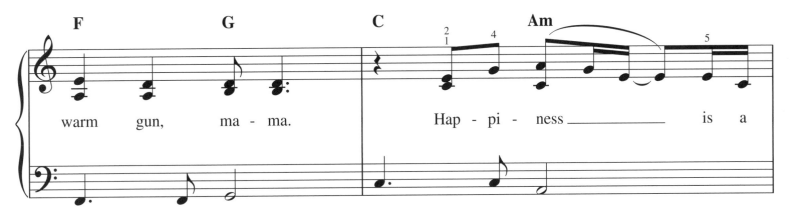

BLACKBIRD

Words and Music by JOHN LENNON
and PAUL McCARTNEY

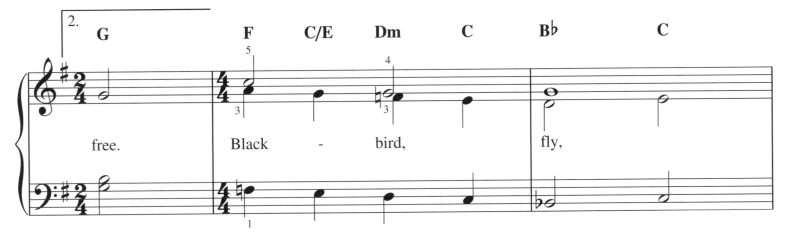

free. Black - bird, fly,

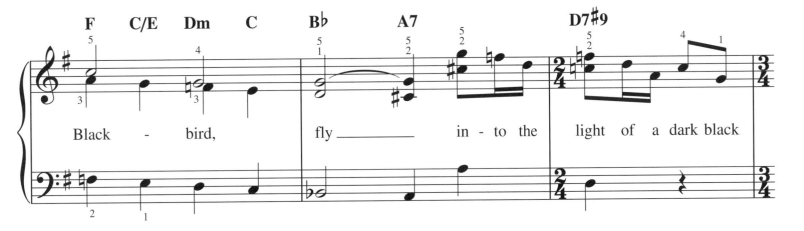

Black - bird, fly _____ in - to the light of a dark black

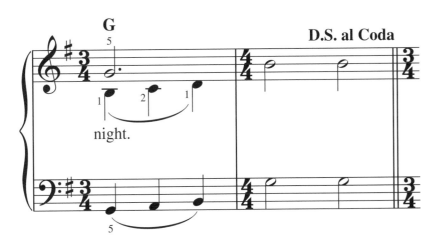

night.

CODA

rise. You were on - ly

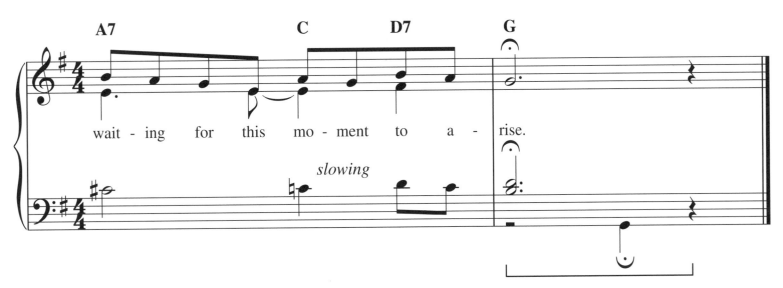

wait - ing for this mo - ment to a - rise.

slowing

HEY JUDE

Words and Music by JOHN LENNON
and PAUL McCARTNEY

Slowly and steadily

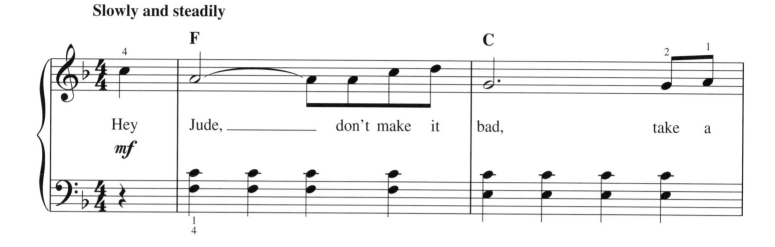

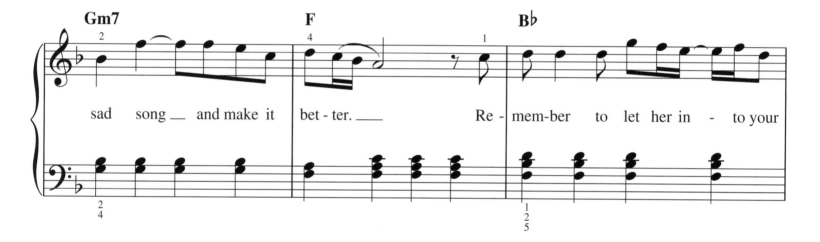

F   **C**   **Gm7**

Jude, _____ don't be a - fraid;   you were made to _____ go out and
Jude, _____ don't let me down;   you have found her, ___ now go and

F   **B♭**

get her. _____   The min - ute you let her un - der your
get her. _____   Re - mem - ber to let her in - to your

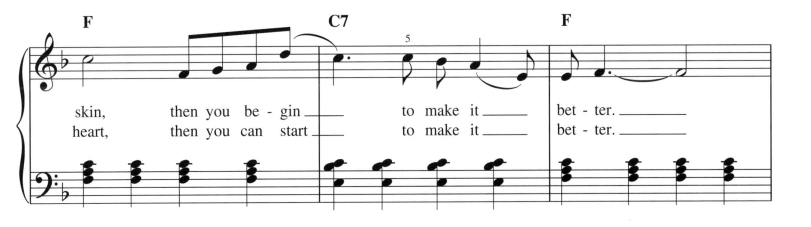

F   **C7**   **F**

skin, then you be - gin ____ to make it ____ bet - ter.
heart, then you can start ____ to make it ____ bet - ter. _____

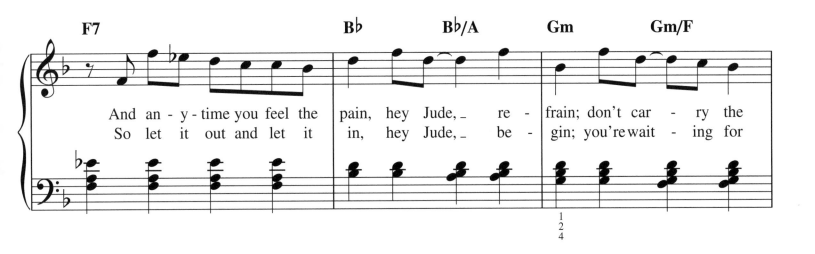

F7   **B♭**   **B♭/A**   **Gm**   **Gm/F**

And an - y - time you feel the pain, hey Jude, _ re - frain; don't car - ry the
So let it out and let it in, hey Jude, _ be - gin; you're wait - ing for

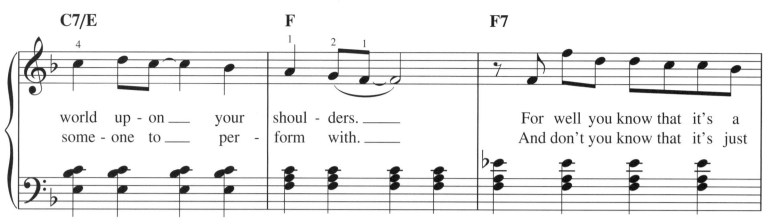

world up - on ___ your shoul - ders. _____
some - one to ___ per - form with. _____

For well you know that it's a
And don't you know that it's just

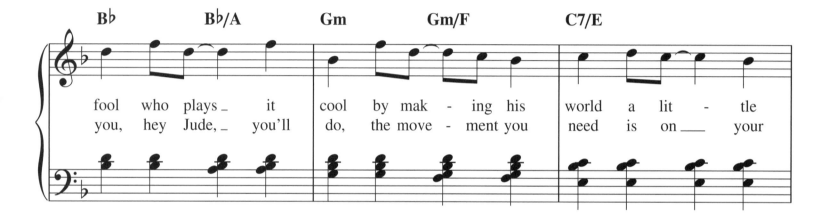

fool who plays ___ it
you, hey Jude, _ you'll

cool by mak - ing his
do, the move - ment you

world a lit - tle
need is on ___ your

cold - er. ___
shoul - der. ___ } Da da da da ___ da da da da da.

1.
Hey

2.
Hey

Jude, _____ don't make it

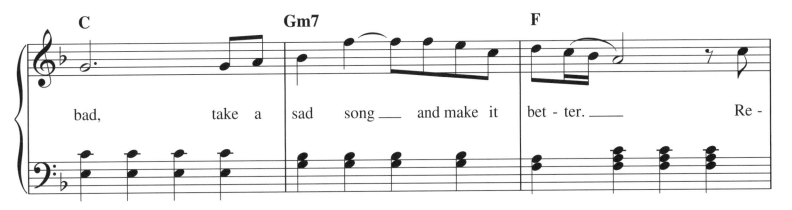

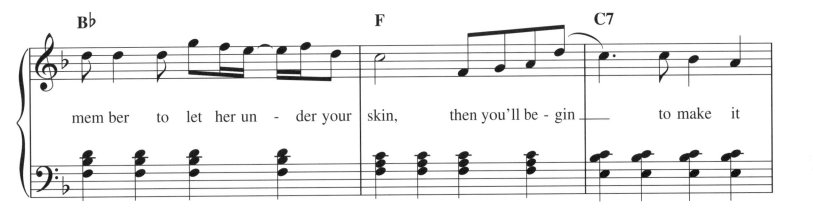

DON'T LET ME DOWN

Words and Music by JOHN LENNON
and PAUL McCARTNEY

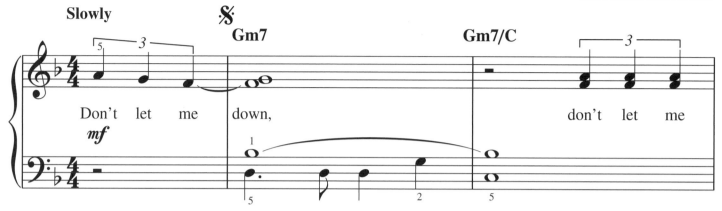

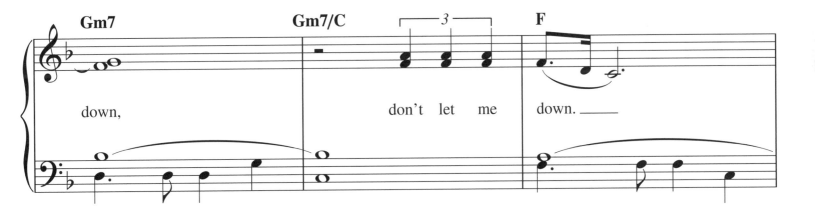

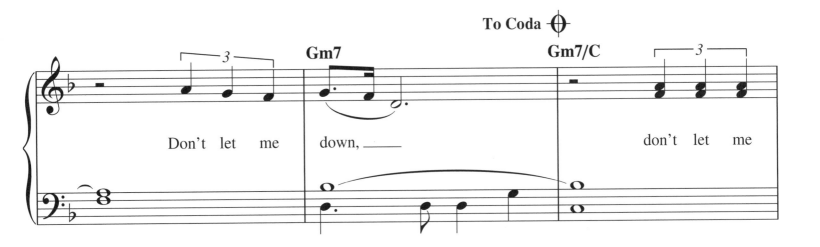

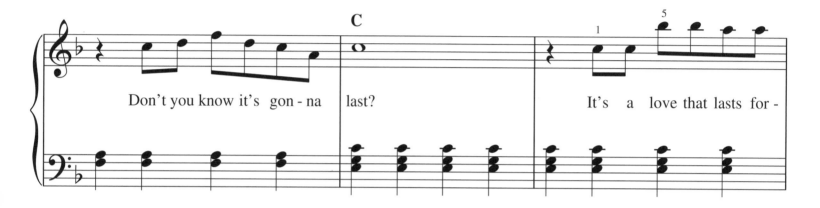

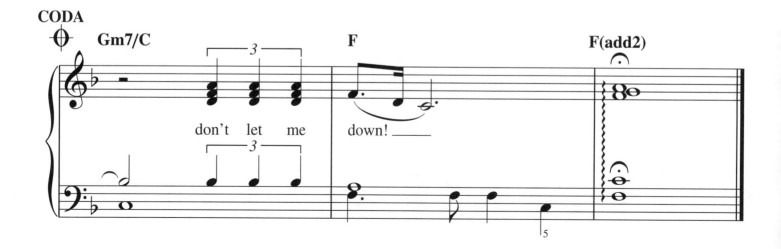

ALL YOU NEED IS LOVE

Words and Music by JOHN LENNON
and PAUL McCARTNEY

Moderately, not too fast

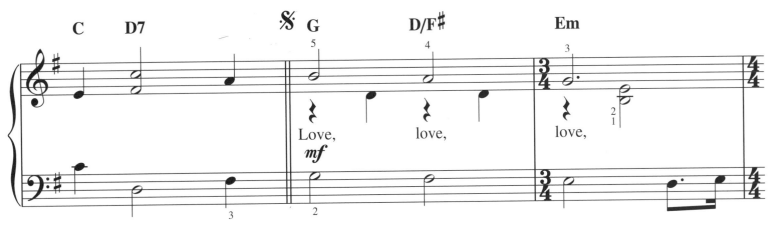

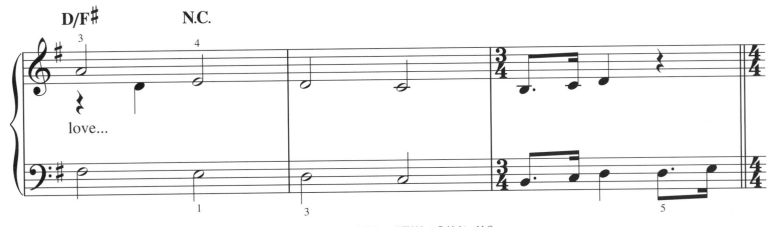

There's noth-ing you can do that can't be done.
Noth-ing you can make that can't be made.
Noth-ing you can know that is-n't known.

Noth-ing you can sing that can't be sung.
No one you can save that can't be saved.
Noth-ing you can see that is-n't shown.

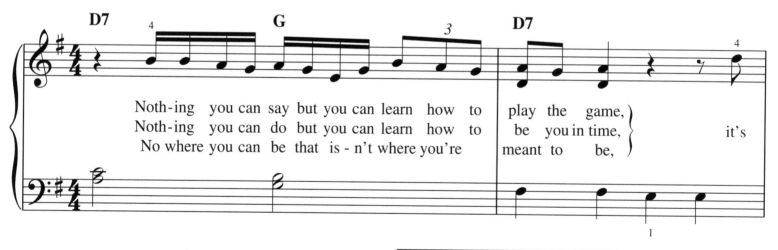

Noth-ing you can say but you can learn how to play the game, it's
Noth-ing you can do but you can learn how to be you in time,
No where you can be that is-n't where you're meant to be,

eas - y.

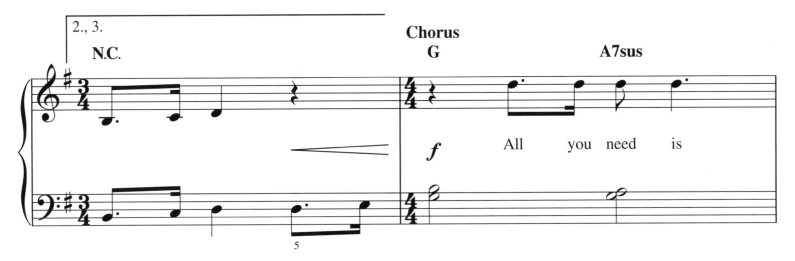

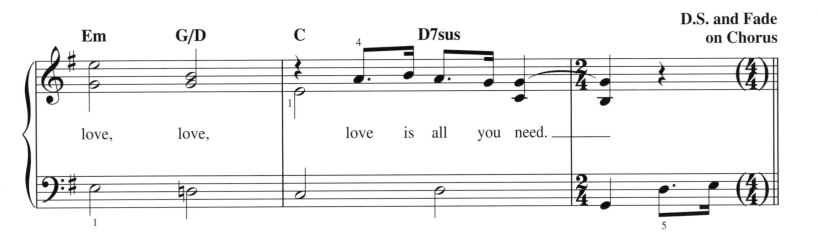

LUCY IN THE SKY WITH DIAMONDS

Words and Music by JOHN LENNON
and PAUL McCARTNEY

Moderately flowing

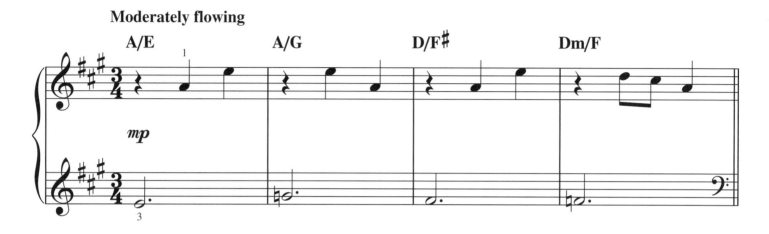

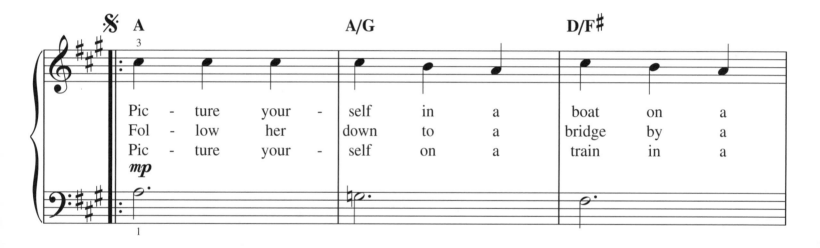

Pic - ture your - self in a boat on a
Fol - low her down to a bridge by a
Pic - ture your - self on a train in a

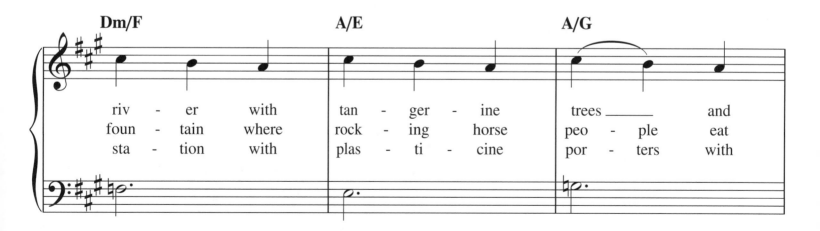

riv - er with tan - ger - ine trees _____ and
foun - tain where rock - ing horse peo - ple eat
sta - tion with plas - ti - cine por - ters with

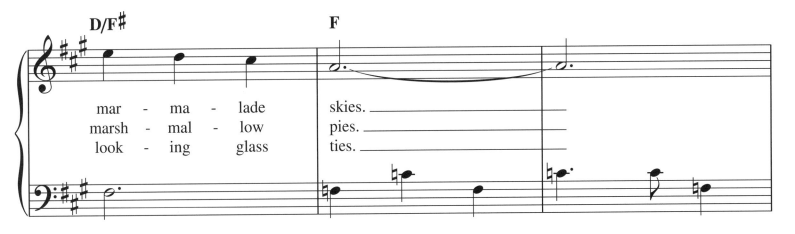

D/F#   **F**

mar - ma - lade | skies. _____
marsh - mal - low | pies. _____
look - ing glass | ties. _____

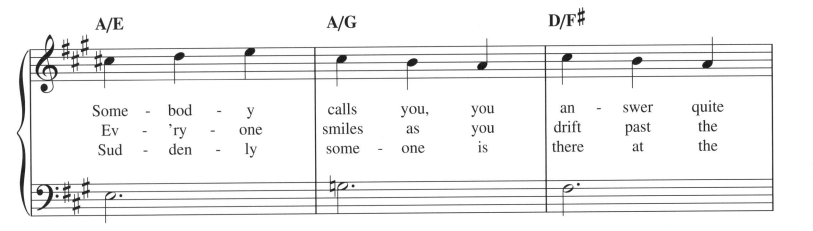

A/E   **A/G**   **D/F#**

Some - bod - y | calls you, you | an - swer quite
Ev - 'ry - one | smiles as you | drift past the
Sud - den - ly | some - one is | there at the

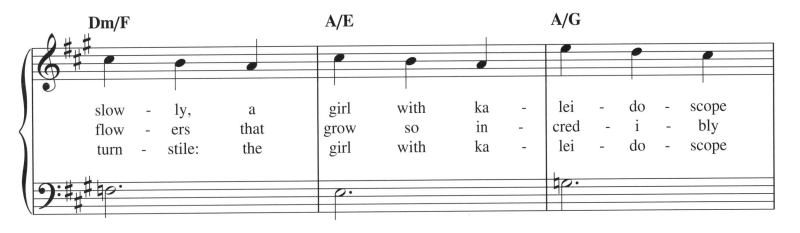

Dm/F   **A/E**   **A/G**

slow - ly, a | girl with ka - | lei - do - scope
flow - ers that | grow so in - | cred - i - bly
turn - stile: the | girl with ka - | lei - do - scope

To Coda ⊕

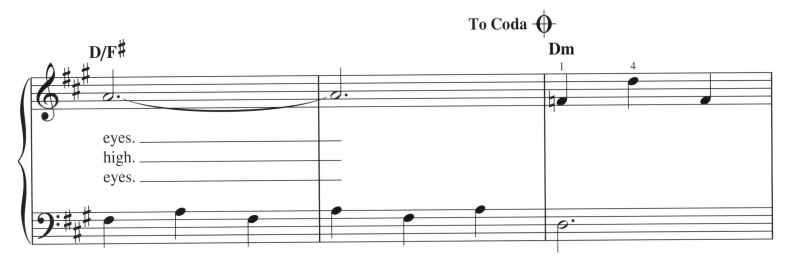

D/F#   **Dm**

1   4

eyes. _____
high. _____
eyes. _____

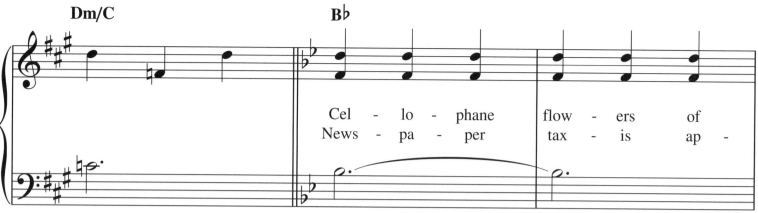

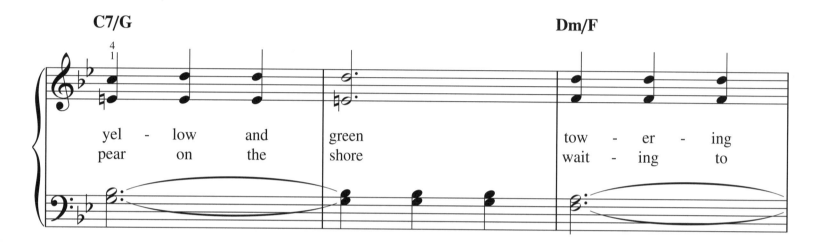

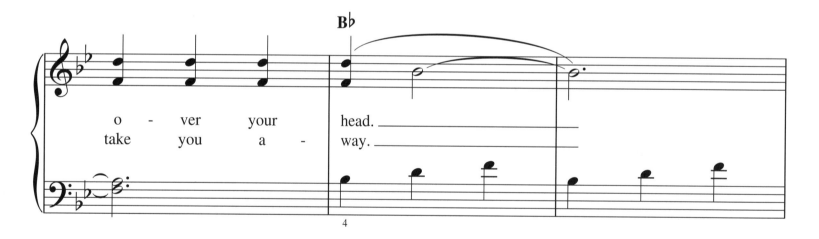

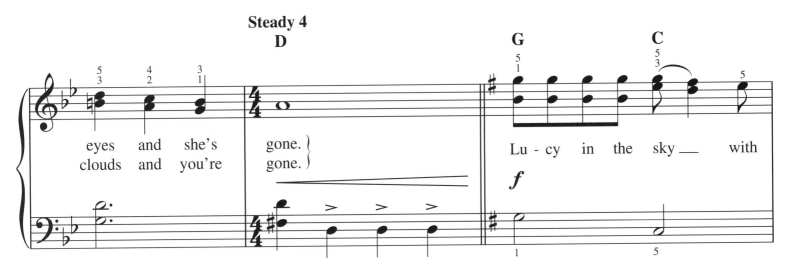

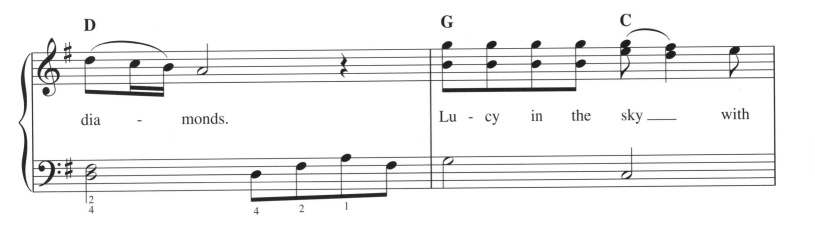

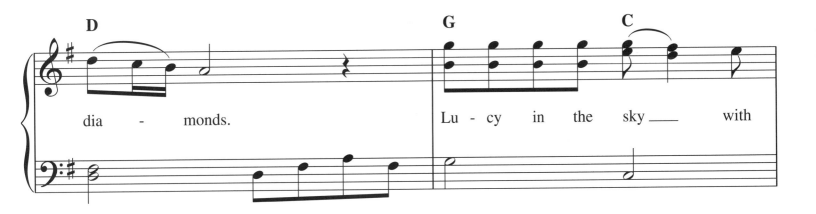

CODA

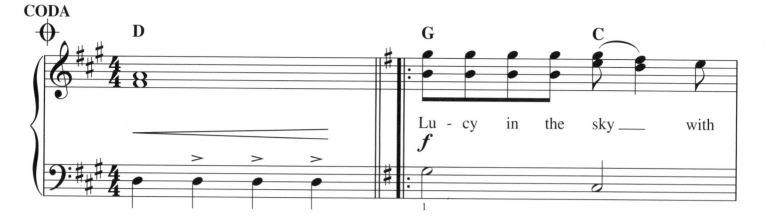

Repeat and Fade